Quick Column Quilts

Make 12+ Bold & Beautiful Designs in Half the Time

Nancy Zieman

C&T PUBLISHING
Another Maker Inspired!

Contents

Introduction

Quilt designs are commonly based on squares, triangles or circles—or a combination thereof. However, there's another word you might want to add to your repertoire of patchwork descriptions: That word is *columns*!

Column quilts are ideal projects for quilting newbies and offer a fresh approach for quilting enthusiasts. The visual impact is modern and the sewing is streamlined.

Crosswise strips of fabric are the main component for the columns, yet a few traditional, simple quilt blocks can be added for interest.

If you have some quilting experience, you're ready for your Quick Column Quilt journey! Just choose from the thirteen column quilt options. If you're new to quilting or want to refresh your skills, turn to the back of the book for recommended supplies and tools and suggested finishing details, including layering, quilting and binding.

Modern. Streamlined. Quick. With characteristics such as these, the column quilt will no doubt soon become your go-to form of patchwork.

42" × 58" (106.7cm × 147.3)

CHAPTER ONE

Heartbeat Column Quilt

No matter the size—baby to king—you can sew this quilt in a heartbeat! Colorful accent strips in a variety of widths make up the heartbeat pattern, while the subdued one-color strips add a perfect background for the design. The quilt shown at left is a tummy-time quilt—a small quilt that is placed on the floor for a baby's "tummy time" exercises.

FINISHED SIZE

- Approximately 42" × 58" (106.7cm × 147.3cm)

SUPPLIES

- ¼ yard (.1m–.2m) each of 8 accent fabrics 1½ yards (1.4m) background fabric
- 1¾ yards (1.6m) of 45" (114.3cm) or wider backing fabric, or pieced fabric measuring 45" × 60" (114.3cm × 152.4cm)
- Crib-size batting (45" × 60"/ 114.3cm × 152.4cm)
- Essential Quilting Tools (see listing on page 110)

NOTE FROM NANCY

Try to cut a variety of widths from each fabric. It is much better if the strips are neither all narrow nor all wide. Listed below are the exact widths of the crosswise strips used to create the featured 42" × 58" (106.7cm × 147.3cm) quilt top.

Orange: 1½" (3.8cm), 2" (5.1cm)
Purple: 1¾" (4.4cm), 2½" (6.4cm)
Light pink: 2" (5.1cm), 4" (10.2cm)
Lime: 1¼" (3.2cm), 4½" (11.4cm)
Blue: 1¾" (4.4cm), 3½" (8.9cm)
Dark green: 2" (5.1cm), 3" (7.6cm), 4½" (11.4cm)
Yellow: 3" (7.6cm), 4¼" (10.8cm)
Dark pink: 1½" (3.8cm), 2" (5.1cm), 4½" (11.4cm)

Note: All seam allowances are ¼" (6mm) unless otherwise stated.

1 PREPARE AND CUT FABRICS

- Stabilize all fabrics well using spray starch or a starch alternative such as Mary Ellen's Best Press. See page 112.
- Cut eighteen to twenty-two 1½"–4½" (3.8cm–11.4cm) crosswise strips (2 or 3 of each color). Cut a narrower and a wider width of each color. See sidebar on this page.
- Cut the same number and same widths of background strips as the colored accent strips. Figure 1.

Figure 1

2 JOIN CROSSWISE ACCENT AND BACKGROUND STRIPS

- Pair a background strip with each accent strip, placing their right sides together.
- Stitch both short ends, thereby creating a tube. Figure 2.
- Stitch ends in a continuous chain stitch to save time. Clip the thread between the strips when it's completed. Press all seams open. Figure 3.

Note: You should have 18 to 20 tube sets. Figure 4.

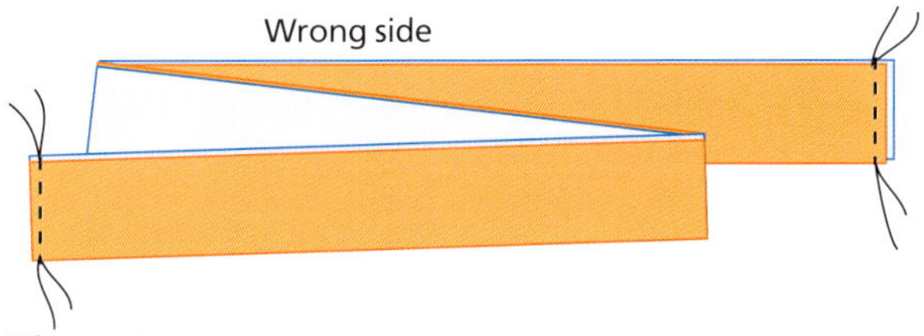

Figure 2

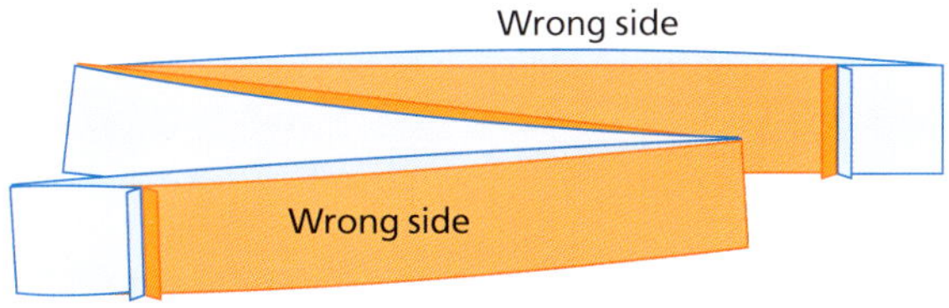

Figure 3

3 DETERMINE THE "HEARTBEAT" LAYOUT

- Fold the fabric tubes in half, alternating the amount of accent color that is visible. Vary the lengths of the visible accent colors. Figure 5.
- Arrange the colors in a pleasing arrangement or refer to the layout guide, Figure 7 on page 10.

Figure 4

4 CUT TUBES IN HALF

- Cut the folds of each strip. To do this, make 1 cut across the accent color, and make the second across the background color.
- Separate the tube. The top side is for the top half of the quilt, and the underneath side is for the lower half of the quilt top. Figure 6.

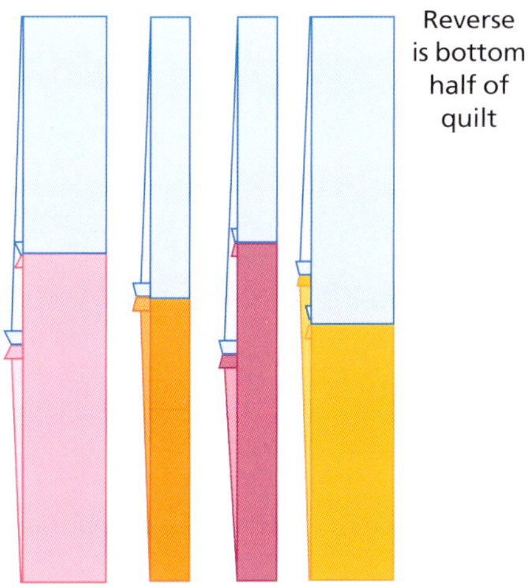

Figure 5

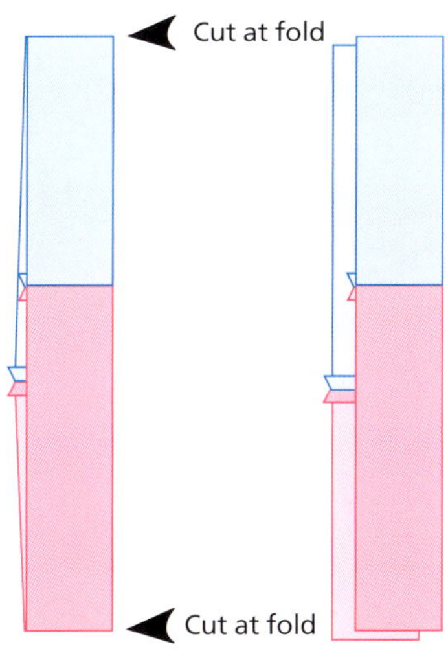

Figure 6

5 COMPLETE THE QUILT TOP

- Stitch the top half of the quilt top in pairs. Press seams open. Figure 7.
- Stitch all pairs to create the top half of the quilt top. Figure 8.
- Rearrange the columns in a different configuration than the top half of the quilt.
- Stitch and press the bottom columns, as detailed for the top half of the quilt. Figure 9.
- Align the top and the lower halves of the quilt top, right sides together; pin and stitch. Press seam open. Figure 10.

6 LAYER, QUILT AND BIND

- Use your favorite methods or refer to pages 114–121.

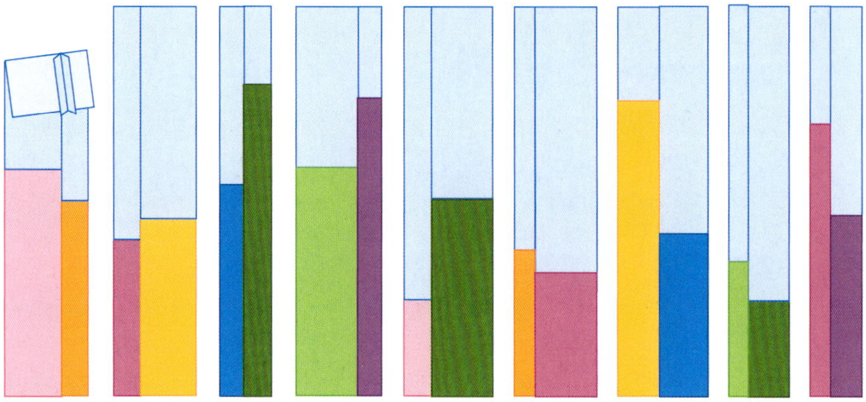
Figure 7

Figure 8

Figure 9

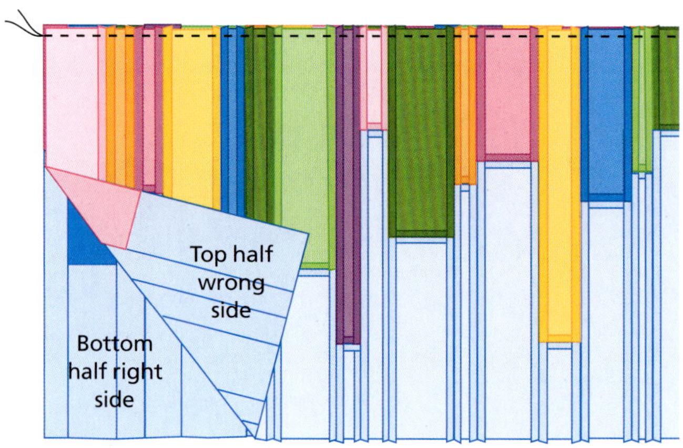

Figure 10

CREATIVE OPTIONS

Fabric colors can change this quilt style from cute to modern. The gray, white and black prints with a gray background say urban and contemporary, while the pastel choices are perfect for kids.

The Heartbeat Column Quilt is also ideal for larger quilts. Just vary the number, width and length of the columns to accommodate the different sizes from double to king.

This quilt is a double/full 82" × 88" (208.3cm × 223.5cm), but it can be made for queen (86" × 93"/ 218.4cm × 236.2cm) and king (93" × 104"/ 236.2cm × 264.2cm).

Cut approximately twenty-one 2½" (6.4cm) to 6½" (16.5cm) crosswise accent strips. Vary the strip lengths. Figure 11.

To create the needed length for larger quilts, the background columns must be longer than one length.

- Double/Full: One crosswise strip plus a quarter length of a strip. Fold one of the strips in fourths; cut along the folds. Stitch a quarter length to each full crosswise strip. Figure 12.
- Queen or King: One crosswise strip plus a half length of a strip. Fold one of the strips in half; cut along the fold. Stitch a half length to each full crosswise strip. Figure 13.

Assemble as detailed in the project. This time the background column strips are not the same length as the accent color strips because of the half strip pieces that are added to the background strips. Figure 14.

Figure 11

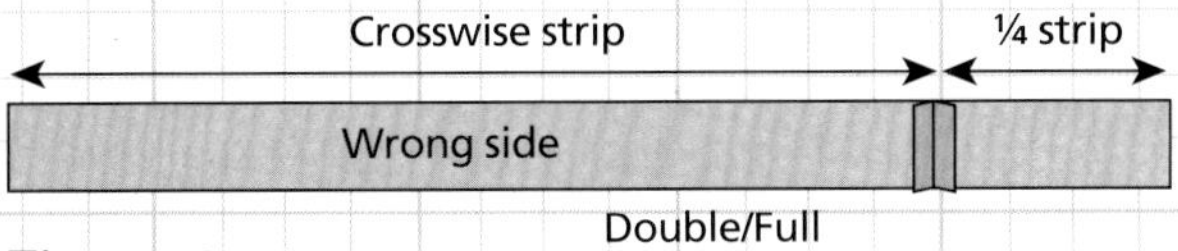

Figure 12

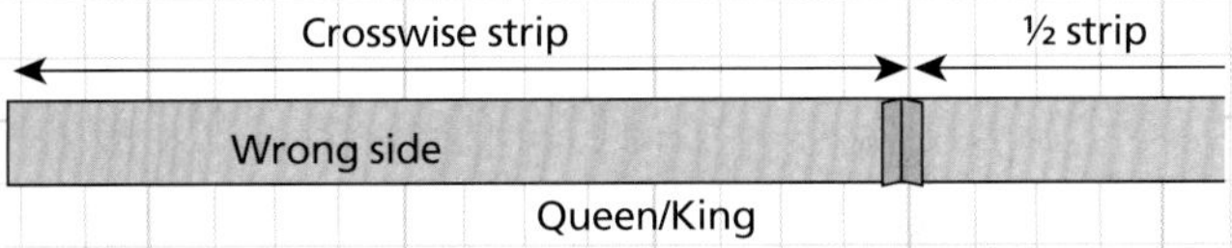

Figure 13

Figure 14

88" × 102" (223.5cm × 259.1cm)

CHAPTER TWO

Interrupted Columns Quilt

This speedy-to-make queen-size quilt is designed with a very easy lesson in color coordination. Simply find a print you love for the sashing, and choose five colors from the print to use for the column colors. The interruptions—horizontal strips—stop the lengthwise movement while creating a more artistic appeal.

FINISHED SIZE

- Approximately 88" × 102" (223.5cm × 259.1cm)

SUPPLIES

- 1 yard (1m) Fabric A (pink) for columns
- ⅝ yard (.6m) Fabric B (orange) for columns
- 1¼ yards (1.1m) Fabric C (aqua) for columns
- 5/8 yard (.6m) Fabric D (red) for columns
- 1¼ yards (1.1m) Fabric E (green) for center column and 2 horizontal strips
- 4¼ yards (3.9m) Fabric F (print) for horizontal and vertical sashing plus binding
- 2⅝ yards (2.4m) backing fabric 106"-wide (269.2cm) or 7⅜ yards (6.7m) backing fabric 42"-wide (106.7cm)
- Queen-size batting
- Essential Quilting Tools (see listing on page 110)

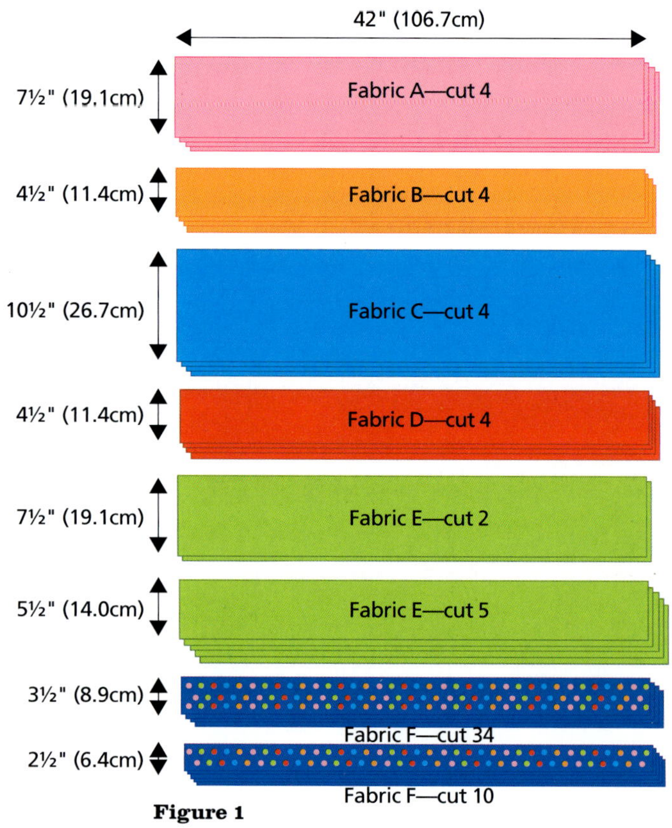

Figure 1

Note: All seam allowances are ¼" (6mm) unless otherwise stated.

1 PREPARE AND CUT FABRICS

- Stabilize all fabrics well using spray starch or a starch alternative such as Mary Ellen's Best Press. See page 112.
- Fabric A (pink) columns: Cut four 7½" (19.1cm) crosswise strips. Figure 1.
- Fabric B (orange) columns: Cut four 4½" (11.4cm) crosswise strips.
- Fabric C (aqua) columns: Cut four 10½" (26.7cm) crosswise strips.
- Fabric D (red) columns: Cut four 4½" (11.4cm) crosswise strips.
- Fabric E (green) center column and 2 rows:
  - Cut two 7½" (19.1cm) crosswise strips (columns).
  - Cut five 5½" (14.0cm) crosswise strips (horizontal strips—set aside).
- Fabric F (print) horizontal and vertical sashing plus binding:
  - Cut thirty-four 3½" (8.9cm) crosswise strips (horizontal and vertical sashing).
  - Cut ten 2½" (6.4cm) strips (binding).

2 CREATE THE VERTICAL COLUMNS

- Pin and stitch sashing strips to left edges of each column strip. On the ninth column, add an additional sashing strip to the right edge.
- Stitch the newly created column strips together following the layout guide for column sets. Figure 2.
- Repeat to stitch 2 identical subsets.

Note: The five 5½" (14.0cm) green column strips are used for the horizontal strips.

- Press seam allowances open or in 1 direction.
- Square the top and bottom edges of the column sets. The column sets should measure approximately 42" × 88" (106.7cm × 223.5cm).
- Cut 1 of the column sets into 2 sections that measure 17" × 88" (43.2cm × 223.5cm). There will be approximately 8" (20.3cm) left over. Figure 2.

Note: The 17" × 88" (43.2cm × 223.5cm) column sections are placed above and below the larger 42" × 88" (43.2cm × 223.5cm) column set. The remaining 8" (20.3cm) section is not used as part of the quilt top. Consider making a scrappy backing, page 114, and include this colorful section as part of the backing.

3 CREATE THE INTERRUPTED COLUMNS

- Piece together the five 5½" (14.0cm) Fabric E (green) crosswise strips, stitching end to end.
- Cut 2 strips, each 88" (223.5cm) long, from the pieced Fabric E strips for the horizontal strips.
- Piece the 14 remaining 3½" (8.9cm) Fabric F (print) crosswise strips, stitching end to end.
- Cut 6 strips, each 88" (223.5cm) long, from the pieced Fabric F for the horizontal sashing. Reserve two 88" (223.5cm) strips for top and bottom borders.
- Stitch a Fabric F strip to the top and bottom of each Fabric E strip. Figure 3.

4 COMPLETE THE QUEEN-SIZE QUILT TOP

- Stitch an interrupted column to the top and bottom of the 42" × 88" (106.7cm × 223.5cm) vertical column set.
- Stitch the shorter 17" × 88" (43.2cm × 223.5cm) vertical column sections to the top and lower edges of the horizontal columns. Figure 4.

5 LAYER, QUILT AND BIND

- Use your favorite methods or refer to pages 114–121.
- Use the Fabric F binding strips for the binding.

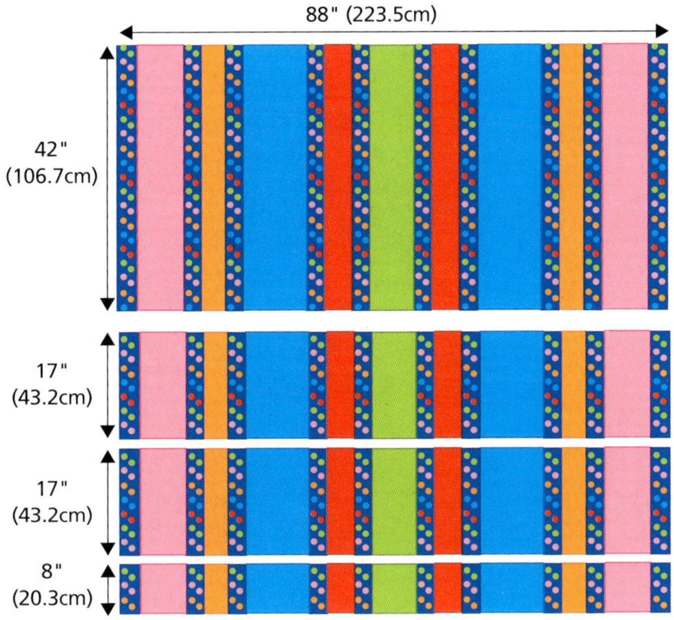

Figure 2

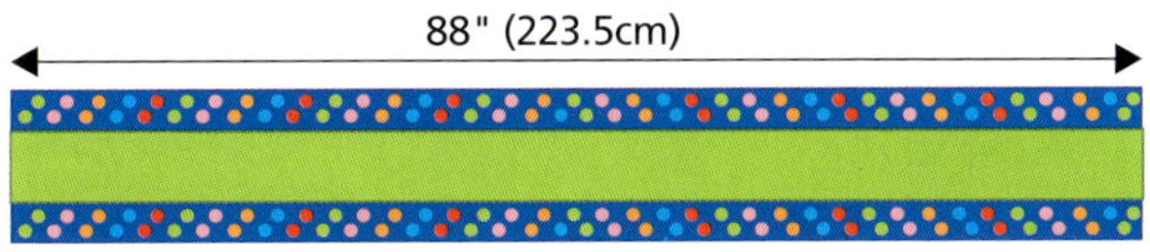

Figure 3

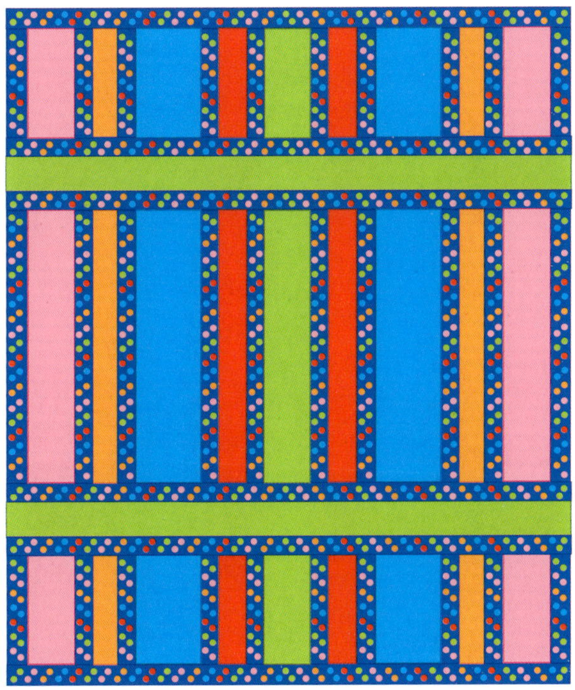

Figure 4

45" × 60" (114.3cm × 152.4cm)

CHAPTER THREE

Carefree Column Quilt

Fat quarters, those convenient fabric cuts approximately 18" × 21" (45.7cm × 53.3cm), are ideal for this next column quilt. Made with six fat quarter cuts and a background fabric, this lap quilt is ideal for bright fabric choices.

FINISHED SIZE

- Approximately 45" × 60" (114.3cm × 152.4cm)

SUPPLIES

- 1 fat quarter (18" × 21" [45.7cm × 53.3cm]) Fabric A (red) for blocks
- 1 fat quarter (18" × 21" [45.7cm × 53.3cm]) Fabric B (orange) for blocks
- 1 fat quarter (18" × 21" [45.7cm × 53.3cm]) Fabric C (yellow) for blocks
- 1 fat quarter (18" × 21" [45.7cm × 53.3cm]) Fabric D (blue) for blocks
- 1 fat quarter (18" × 21" [45.7cm × 53.3cm]) Fabric E (turquoise) for blocks
- 1 fat quarter (18" × 21" [45.7cm × 53.3cm]) Fabric F (green) for blocks
- 1½ yards (1.4m) Fabric G (white) for four-patch blocks, narrow columns, binding and borders
- 1¾ yards (1.6m) Fabric H, at least 44" wide (111.8cm) for backing
- 2 yards (1.8m) batting
- Essential Quilting Tools (see listing on page 110)

Note: All seam allowances are ¼" (6mm) unless otherwise stated.

1 PREPARE FABRICS

- Stabilize all fabrics well using spray starch or a starch alternative such as Mary Ellen's Best Press. See page 112.

2 CUT FABRICS A–F

- Cut two 6½" × 21" (16.5cm × 53.3cm) rectangles from each A–F fat quarter.
  - Subcut one 6½" × 20" (16.5cm × 50.8cm) rectangle from each A–F fat quarter.
  - Subcut one 6½" × 10" (16.5cm × 25.4cm) rectangle from each A–F fat quarter.
  - Subcut one 6½" × 5" (16.5cm × 12.7cm) rectangle from each A–F fat quarter.
  - Subcut two 6½" × 2½" (16.5cm × 6.4cm) rectangles from each A–F fat quarter.
- Cut one 3½" × 21" (8.9cm × 53.3cm) strip from each of the remaining A–F fat quarters. Subcut four 3½" (8.9cm) squares from each. Figure 1.

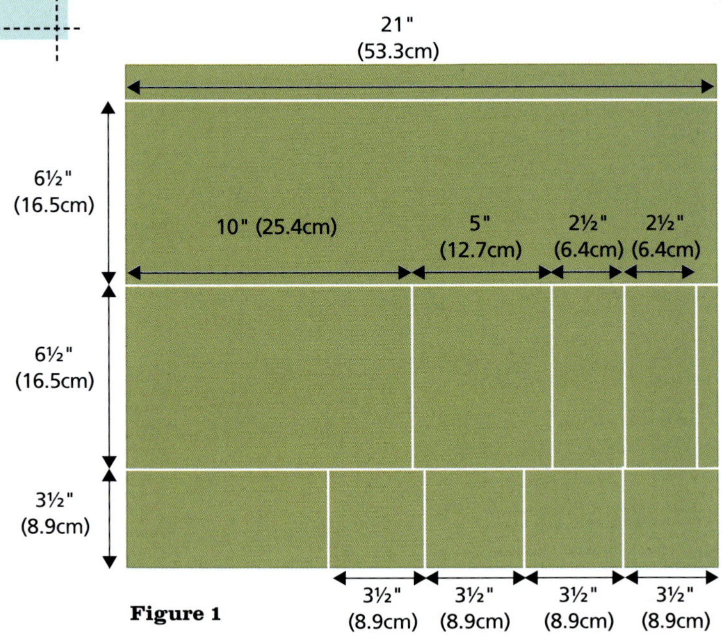

Figure 1

3 CUT FABRIC G

- Cut five 2½" (6.4cm) crosswise strips for the binding.
- Cut nineteen 1½" (3.8cm) crosswise strips for the narrow columns and borders.
  - Set aside 5 of the 1½" (3.8cm) crosswise strips for borders.
  - Subcut six 1½" (3.8cm) crosswise strips into thirty-six 1½" × 6½" (3.8cm × 16.5cm) rectangles for horizontal sashing.
- Stitch eight 1½" (3.8cm) crosswise strips of Fabric G into 1 long strip using diagonal seams. This will be subcut later for vertical sashing. Figure 2.
- Cut three 3½" (8.9cm) crosswise strips (four-patch blocks) of Fabric G. Subcut twenty-four 3½" (8.9cm) squares.

4 POSITION AND JOIN FOUR-PATCH BLOCKS

- Stack each 3½" (8.9cm) square of Fabrics A–F with a 3½" (8.9cm) square of Fabric G, right sides together.
- Join the 24 sections, right sides together and chain stitch the sections.
- Press seams toward Fabrics A–F. Cut chain stitching apart between stitched sections. Figure 3.
- Align and join 2 sets of the same color combination, right sides together, with opposite colors facing each other. Press seams open. Figure 4.

5 ARRANGE THE COLUMNS

- Place like sizes in stacks with the exception of creating 2 identical stacks of the smallest rectangles. Figure 5.
- Use a design wall to arrange 6 columns.
- Start by randomly placing the largest rectangles on the design wall, 1 rectangle per column.

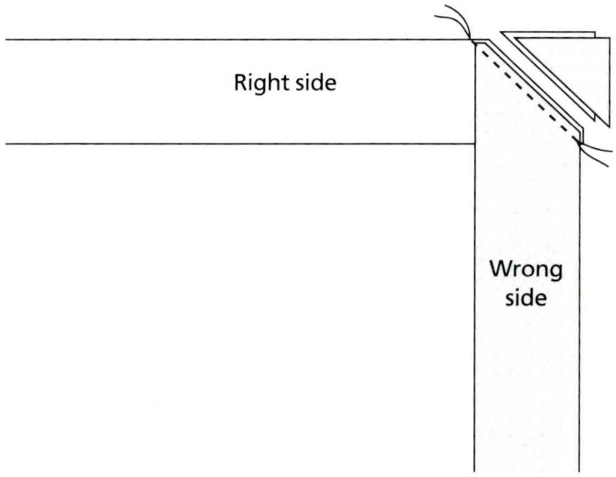

Figure 2

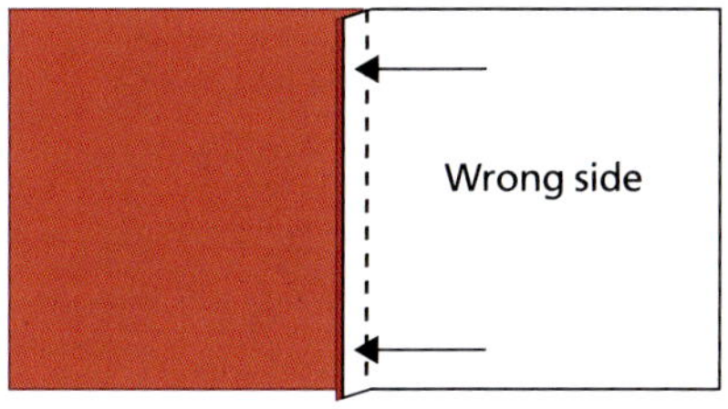

Figure 3

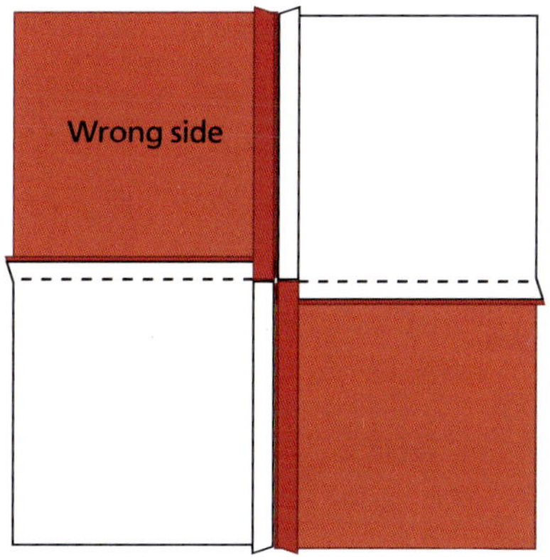

Figure 4

Figure 5

- Fill in the columns with the remaining rectangles. The smallest rectangle will be used twice per column.
- Add 2 different colorations of the four-patches to each column. Figure 6.

6 ADD HORIZONTAL SASHING

- Add a 1½" × 6½" (3.8cm × 16.5cm) sashing strip between the rectangles and four-patches. Work on 1 column at a time.
- Join and press the seams toward the rectangles and four-patches. Repeat stitching for each column.

7 ADD NARROW COLUMNS

- Measure the completed column and cut 5 strips according to that measurement from the Fabric G that you pieced together for vertical sashing in Step 3.
- Align the strips to the right edges of the first, second, third, fourth and fifth columns, right sides together. Pin and stitch sashing strips. Press seams toward the pieced column. Figure 7.
- Join the columns. Press seams toward the pieced columns.

NOTE FROM NANCY

For ease, the illustrations detail the exact layout of the featured quilt.

Figure 6

Figure 7

Note: Seams are pressed toward the pieced columns because the sashing is light. If you use a dark sashing, press seams toward the sashing.

8 ADD BORDERS

- Measure the top edge of the quilt, and cut 2 of the reserved 1½" (3.8cm) lengths of Fabric G border strips to this length.
- Stitch these fabric strips to the top and bottom of the quilt. Figure 8.
- Measure the side edges of the quilt, and cut 2 of the reserved 1½" (3.8cm) Fabric G border strips to this length. Cut part of the fifth Fabric G border strip, if needed, for each piece, and join strips diagonally to obtain the total length needed.
- Stitch remaining borders to the side edges of the quilt. Figure 9.

9 LAYER, QUILT AND BIND

- Use your favorite methods or refer to pages 114–121.

Figure 8

Figure 9

80" × 88" (203.2cm × 223.5cm)

CHAPTER FOUR

Wind Chime Column Quilt

The beautiful wind chimes that hang from our deck served as the inspiration for this column quilt. Just like the real wind chimes, the angled accent pieces move as if gently nudged by a breeze.

FINISHED SIZE

- Approximately 80" × 88" (203.2cm × 223.5cm)

SUPPLIES

- ⅛–½ yard (.1m–.5m) Fabrics A–F. (See Step 1 on how to audition fabric from your fabric stash.)
- 4⅝ yards (4.2m) Fabric G 42"-wide (106.7cm) for background, narrow columns
- ¾ yard (.7m) Fabric H for binding
- 2⅝ yards (2.4m) backing fabric 108"-wide (274.3cm) or 5¼ yards (4.8m) backing fabric 42"-wide (106.7cm). Or see scrappy backing options, page 114.
- Queen-size batting
- Essential Quilting Tools (see listing on page 110)

NOTE FROM NANCY

This is a great stash-buster quilt! I created the wind chime accents from my leftover fabrics; only the aqua (background) fabric was purchased specifically for this quilt. Some of the fabrics used in the featured quilt were fat quarters (18" × 21" [45.7cm × 53.3cm]) or smaller, while other fabrics were ⅛–¼ of a yard (.1m–.2m). In other words, if you have small pieces of fabrics, you can certainly use them.

Note: All seam allowances are ¼" (6mm) unless otherwise stated.

1 AUDITION THE FABRIC FOR THE WIND CHIME ACCENTS

- From your fabric stash, select a print that has a variety of colors to serve as the inspiration to select other fabrics for the quilt. The striped fabric was the inspirational fabric for this quilt.
- Audition fabrics from your fabric stash to coordinate with the inspirational fabric. Figure 1.
- Select a solid background fabric.

2 CUT THE BACKGROUND AND BINDING FABRICS

- Cut thirty-one 2½" (6.4cm) crosswise strips from the background fabric for the narrow columns.
- Cut five 2½" (6.4cm) crosswise strips, five 4½" (11.4cm) crosswise strips, and six 6½" (16.5cm) crosswise strips from the background fabric for the wind chime columns.
- Cut nine 2½" (6.4cm) crosswise strips from the binding fabric. Figure 2.

Figure 1

3 CUT THE FABRIC FOR THE WIND CHIME ACCENTS

- Cut 6 to 7 different 2½" (6.4cm) crosswise cuts from various accent fabrics.
- Cut 7 to 8 different 4½" (11.4cm) crosswise cuts from various accent fabrics.
- Cut 7 to 8 different 6½" (16.5cm) crosswise cuts from various accent fabrics. Figure 3.

4 SEW THE ANGLED WIND CHIME STRIPS

- Sew each wind chime strip in a circle. Meet short ends and right sides. Stitch with a ¼" (6mm) seam allowance.
- Chain stitch the fabrics together. Figure 4.
- Clip the threads between the chain stitching to separate the units.
- Press the seams open. Figure 5.
- Lay each fabric circle on a cutting mat. Separate the layers, keeping 1 long edge aligned with a horizontal mark on the cutting mat.
- Align the 45° mark of the ruler along the straight edge of the fabric. Cut the strip in half. Figure 6.

NOTE FROM NANCY

I recommend cutting the darkest fabrics for the narrowest crosswise strips (2½" [6.4cm]). Intense color pops in smaller doses without becoming too overwhelming.

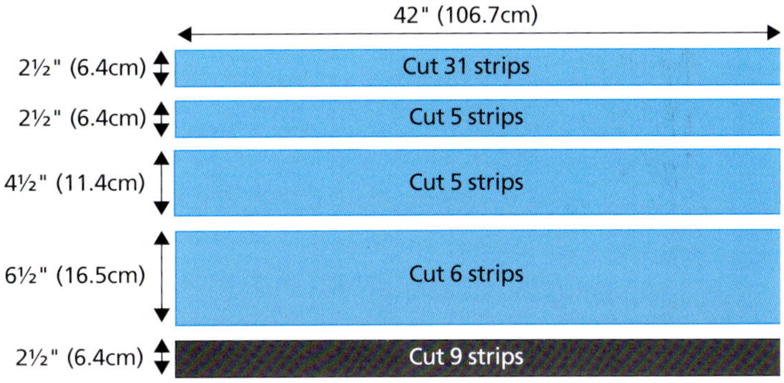

Figure 2

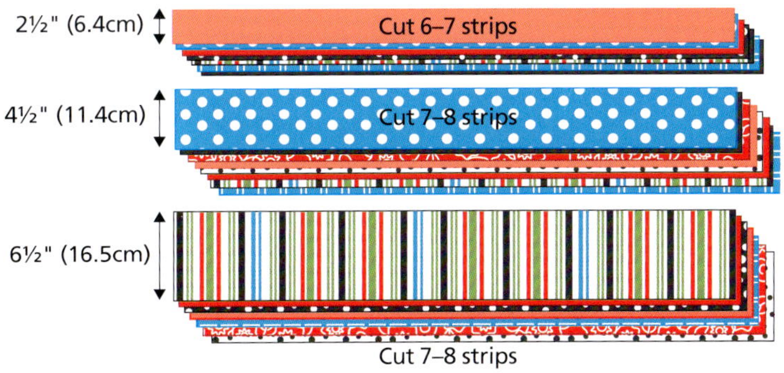

Figure 3

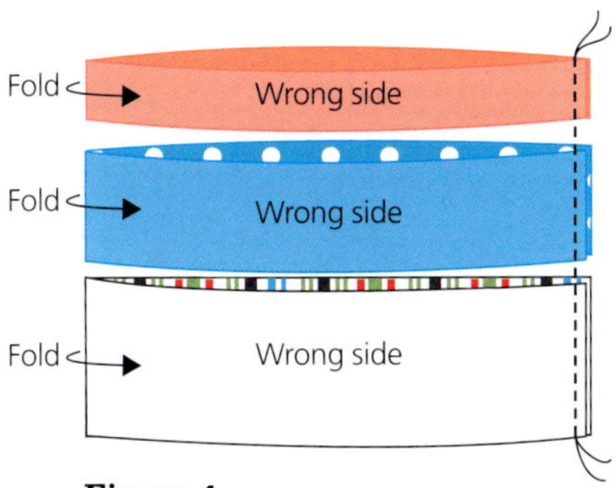

Figure 4

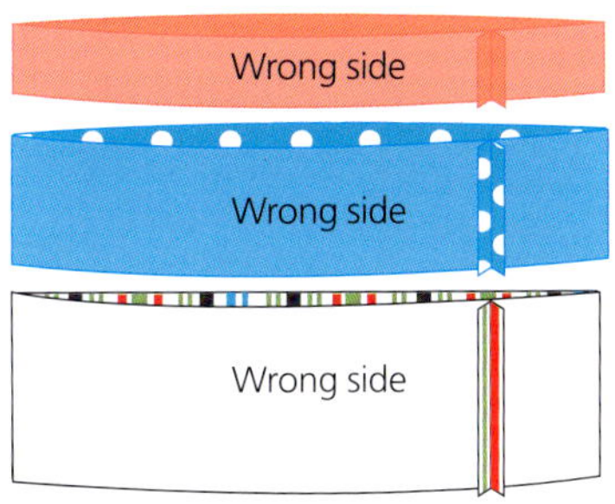

Figure 5

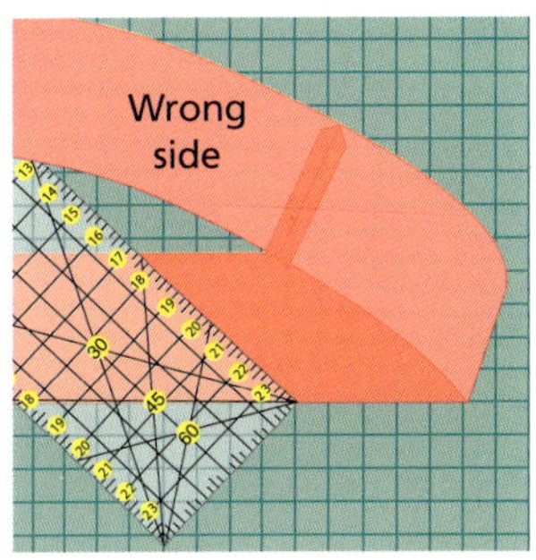

Figure 6

- Cut each length in 2 pieces. Align the fabric along a vertical marking on the cutting mat. Using the same 45° angle, make cuts at approximately one-half, one-third or one-quarter of the length. Make certain that the angle of the ruler doesn't change. Notice that the angles are going in the same direction. Figure 7.

5 SEW THE ANGLED BACKGROUND STRIPS

Repeat the process as stated for the angled windchime strips for the background (aqua) strips.

- Sew each background strip in a circle. Meet short ends and right sides. Stitch with a ¼" (6mm) seam allowance. Figure 8.
- Chain stitch the fabrics together.
- Clip the threads between the chain stitching to separate the units. Press the seams open.
- Lay each fabric circle on a cutting mat. Separate the layers, keeping one long edge aligned with a horizontal mark on the cutting mat.
- Align the 45° mark of the ruler along the straight edge of the fabric. Cut the strip.
- As instructed above, align the fabric along a vertical marking on the cutting mat. Using the same 45° angle, make cuts at approximately one-half, one-third or one-quarter of the length. There is not a specific length measurement. Figure 9.

Note: It might be wise to roughly determine the lengths of the columns (see next step) and leave spaces for the background fabric. Then cut the lengths of the background fabric to achieve the required column lengths.

6 LAY OUT WIND CHIME COLUMNS

- On a large surface (an extended table or the floor), lay out the angle-cut fabrics, alternating a wind chime length with the background length. Begin some of the columns with a wind chime fabric and others with the background fabric. The featured quilt has the following number of columns:
  - Four 2½" (6.4cm) columns
  - Four 4½" (11.4cm) columns
  - Five 6½" (16.5cm) columns

NOTE FROM NANCY

The reason for seaming the strips and then cutting a 45° angle, rather than cutting each end at a 45° angle, is to conserve fabric. With this technique, there is very little fabric waste!

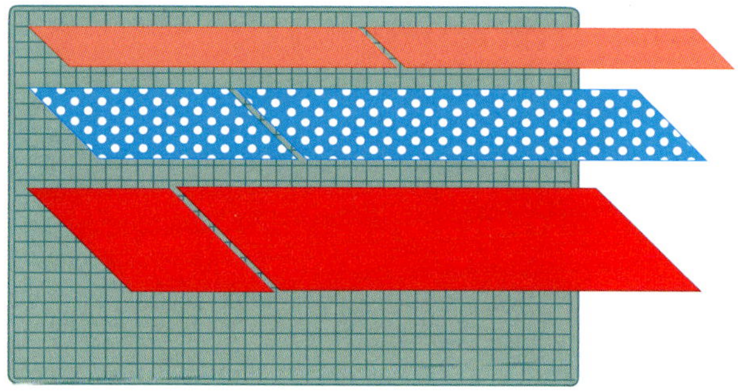

Figure 7

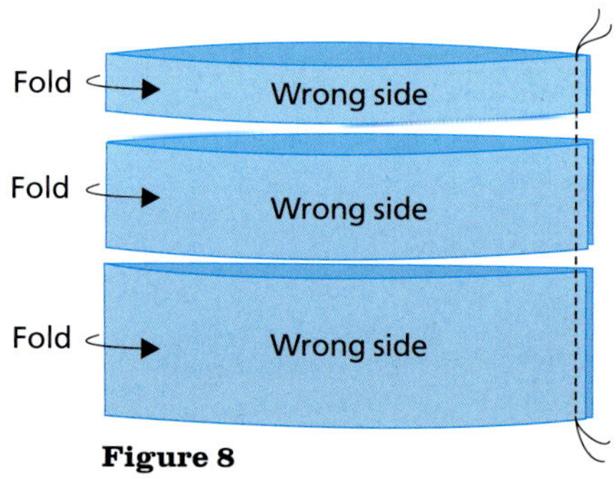

Figure 8

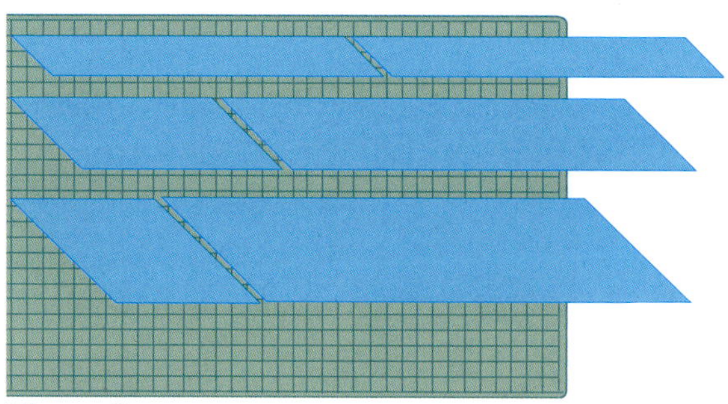

Figure 9

- Alternate the column widths, placing a 4½" (11.4cm) column next to a 2½" (6.4cm) column, which is next to a 6½" (16.5cm) column, etc.
- Mix and match fabrics until the length of the unsewn columns is 90" (228.6cm) or longer. Figure 10.

7 STITCH THE WIND CHIME COLUMNS

- With right sides together, overlap the ends of the column pieces by extending each end ¼" (6mm) beyond the other; pin.
- Stitch the column pieces together. A *V* shape will form. Press the seams open. Figure 11.
- Square the top end of each column, aligning the ruler at a 90° angle, and trim off the excess fabric. Carefully measure down 88" (223.5cm) and trim off the excess length. Figure 12.

8 CREATE THE NARROW COLUMNS

- Stitch the 2½" (6.4cm) narrow columns of background fabric together, end to end. Press seam allowances open.
- Cut long strips into 88" (223.5cm) lengths and create a total of 14 narrow columns.

NOTE FROM NANCY

This layout creates a double-size quilt. Make it larger or smaller by changing the number of columns and the length of the columns. See page 113 for quilt-size guidelines.

Figure 10

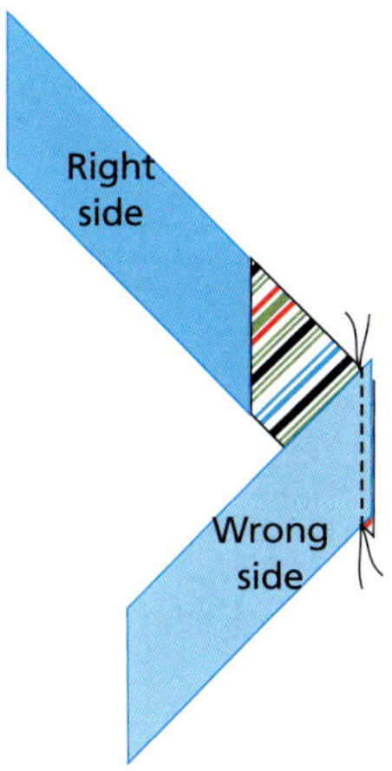

Figure 11

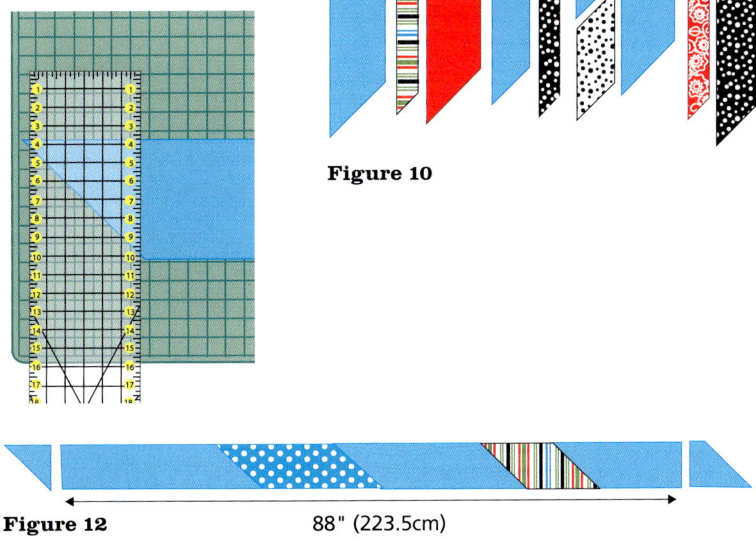

Figure 12

- Lay out the columns between the chime columns, plus add a narrow column along each side edge. Figure 13.

9 STITCH THE COLUMNS

- Stitch the far left narrow column to the far left wind chime column to create a pair. Repeat until 13 pairs have been sewn. Figure 14.
- Stitch the remaining narrow column to the last column pair. Figure 15.
- Press the seam allowances toward the narrow columns. Figure 16.
- Stitch the pairs together to create the quilt top. Figure 17.

10 LAYER, QUILT AND BIND

- Use your favorite methods or refer to pages 114–121.

NOTE FROM NANCY

It might be cumbersome to handle 31 strips that have been sewn together end to end. Consider stitching 3 strips together at a time, press the seams open, and cut an 88" (223.5cm) strip. Then add 2 to 3 more strips to the remaining portion of the strip; again cut an 88" (223.5cm) length. Repeat the process until 14 narrow columns have been cut. (The purpose of joining the strips end to end is to avoid fabric waste.)

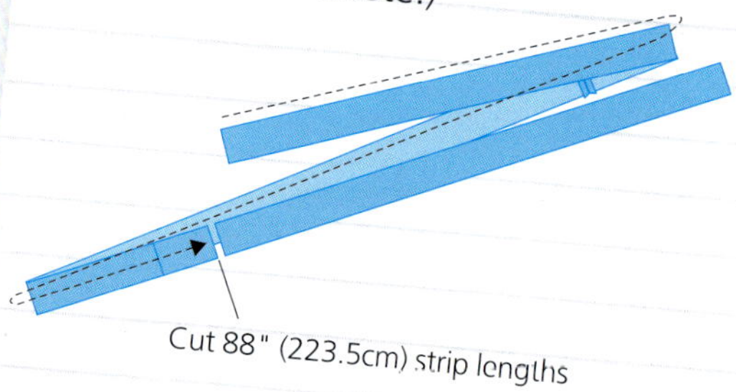

Figure 13

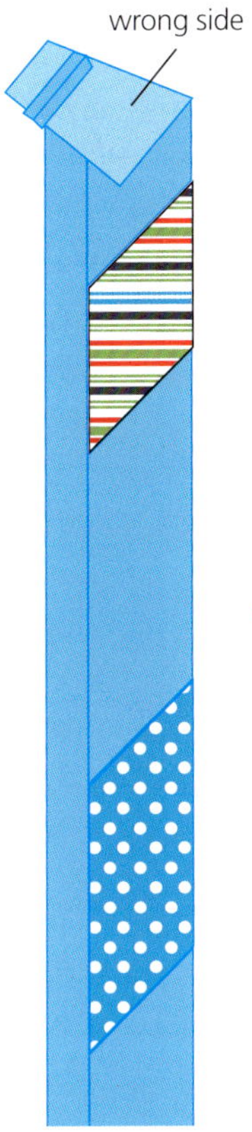

Figure 14

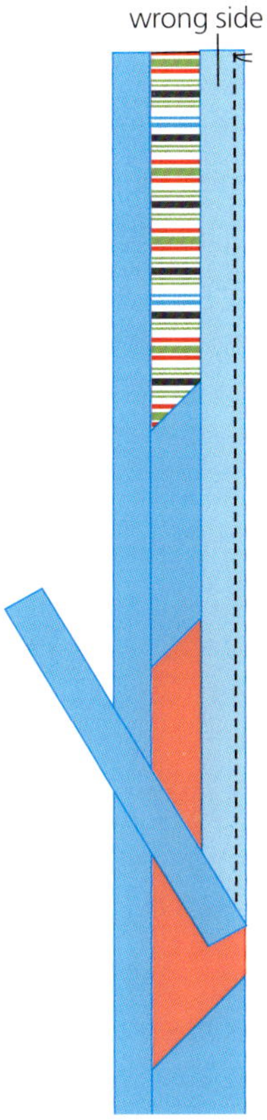

Figure 15

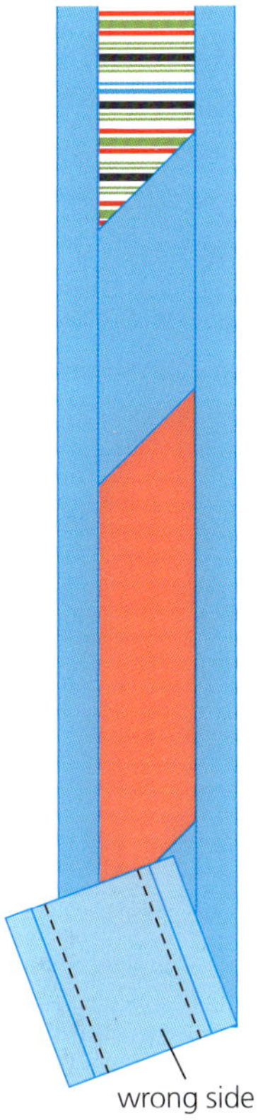

Figure 16

Figure 17

35" × 42" (88.9cm × 106.7cm)

CHAPTER FIVE

Folded Flying Geese Wall Hanging

No half-square triangles are needed to make these artistic Flying Geese. Use prairie points (folded triangles) to create the three-dimensional Flying Geese, and change the size and direction of the geese with ease.

FINISHED SIZE

- Approximately 35" × 42" (88.9cm × 106.7cm)

SUPPLIES

- 6 fat quarters (18" × 21" [45.7cm × 53.3cm]) Fabrics A–F for Flying Geese
- ⅛ yard (.1m) Fabric G for inner borders
- 1⅝ yards (1.5m) Fabric H for background and outer borders
- 1¼ yards (1.1m) Fabric I or muslin for backing
- 1¼ yards (1.1m) batting
- Essential Quilting Tools (see listing on page 110)

Note: All seam allowances are ¼" (6mm) unless otherwise stated.

1 PREPARE FABRICS

- Stabilize all fabrics well using spray starch or a starch alternative, such as Mary Ellen's Best Press. See page 112.

2 CUT SQUARES FOR FLYING GEESE

- Stack the 3 fat quarter fabrics that are used most frequently (red [Fabric A], medium green [Fabric D] and multicolor green [Fabric E]).
  - Cut the layers into 6" (15.2cm), 5" (12.7cm), 4" (10.2cm), 3" (7.6cm) and 2" (5.1cm) strips. Figure 1.
  - Subcut each strip into 6" (15.2cm), 5" (12.7cm), 4" (10.2cm), 3" (7.6cm) and 2" (5.1cm) squares. Figure 2.
- Stack the remaining 3 fat quarter fabrics (gold [Fabric B], green [Fabric C] and gold print [Fabric F]).
  - Cut the layers into strips that are 5" (12.7cm), 4" (10.2cm), 3" (7.6cm) and 2" (5.1cm).

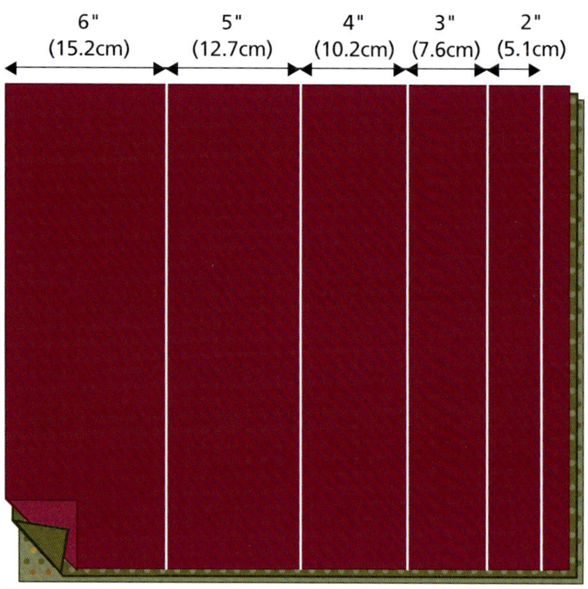

Figure 1

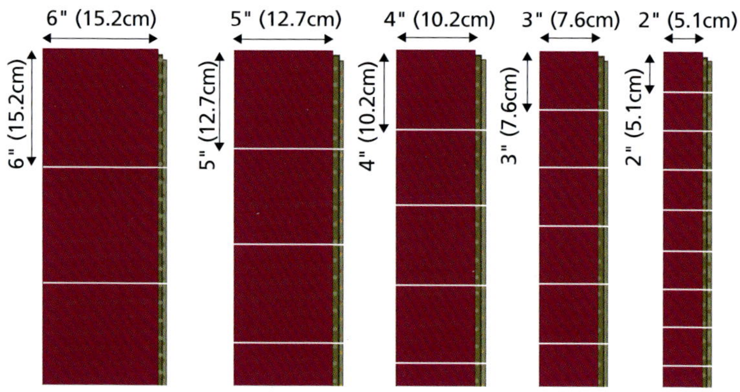

Figure 2

– Subcut each strip into 5" (12.7cm), 4" (10.2cm), 3" (7.6cm) and 2" (5.1cm) squares.

Note: You'll have more squares than you need for this project. Use the extra squares for another project or make the wall hanging larger!

3 CUT AND PREPARE THE BACKGROUND FABRIC H

- Cut the following strips from Fabric H:
  - One 2½" (6.4cm) crosswise strip
  - Two 3½" (8.9cm) crosswise strips
  - One 4½" (11.4cm) crosswise strip
  - Two 5½" (14.0cm) crosswise strips
  - One 6½" (16.5cm) crosswise strip
- Arrange strips and mark placement lines on them with a marking pen and ruler following Figure 3.

NOTE FROM NANCY

To make this step much easier, randomly place the prairie points (see next page) on the columns. The illustrations depict the featured wall hanging, but you're welcome to personalize the design.

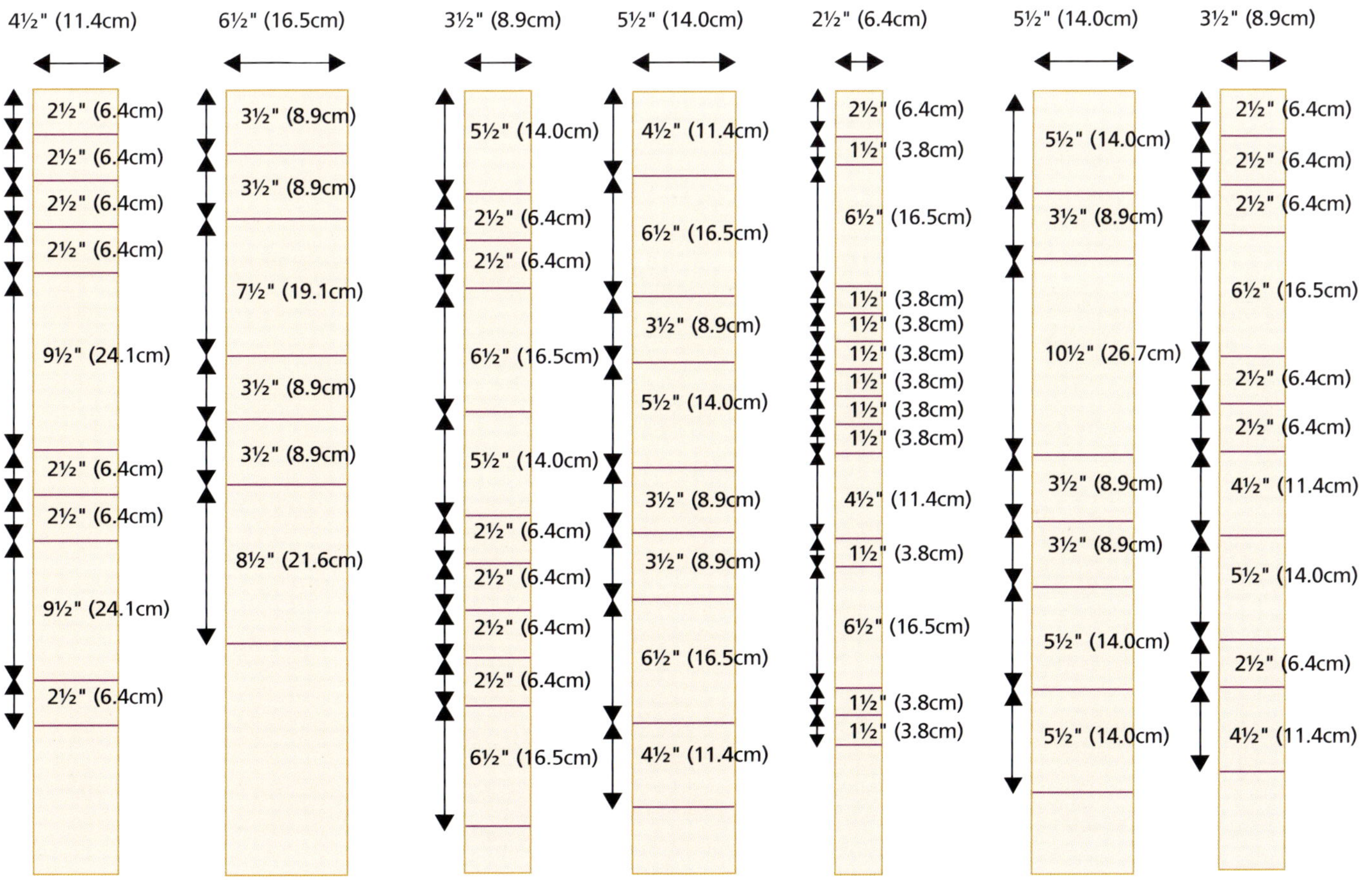

Figure 3

4 MAKE THE PRAIRIE POINTS

- Press all cut squares of Fabrics A–F in half on the grain line, wrong sides together. Figure 4.

Note: Press on the grain for better results when folding the squares to create the prairie points. Cross-grain folds may bow at the tip of the prairie points.

- Meet 1 corner of the folded edge to the cut edge and form a point. Press. Figure 5.
- Meet the second corner of the folded edge to the cut edge. Press. Figure 6.
- Repeat for all prairie points with Fabrics A–F.

5 PREPARE COLUMNS FOR THE QUILT

- Column 1: Center and pin 4" (10.2cm) prairie points *facing down* on the background strip, as shown.
  - Insert 4 Fabric A (red) prairie points.
  - Insert 3 Fabric B (gold) prairie points.
  - Insert 2 Fabric C (green) prairie points. Figure 7.
- Column 2: Center and pin 6" (15.2cm) prairie points *facing down* on the background strip, as shown.
  - Insert 2 Fabric D (medium green print) prairie points.
  - Insert 3 Fabric E (multicolor green print) prairie points.
  - Insert 1 Fabric A (red) prairie point. Figure 8.
- Column 3: Center and pin 3" (7.6cm) prairie points *facing up* on the background strip, as shown.
  - Insert 3 Fabric B (gold) prairie points.
  - Insert 1 Fabric C (green) prairie point.
  - Insert 5 Fabric A (red) prairie points.
  - Insert 1 Fabric E (multicolor green) prairie point. Figure 9.
- Column 4: Center and pin 5" (12.7cm) prairie points *facing down* on the background strip, as shown.
  - Insert 2 Fabric C (green) prairie points.
  - Insert 2 Fabric A (red) prairie points.
  - Insert 3 Fabric B (gold) prairie points.
  - Insert 1 Fabric D (medium green print) prairie point. Figure 10.

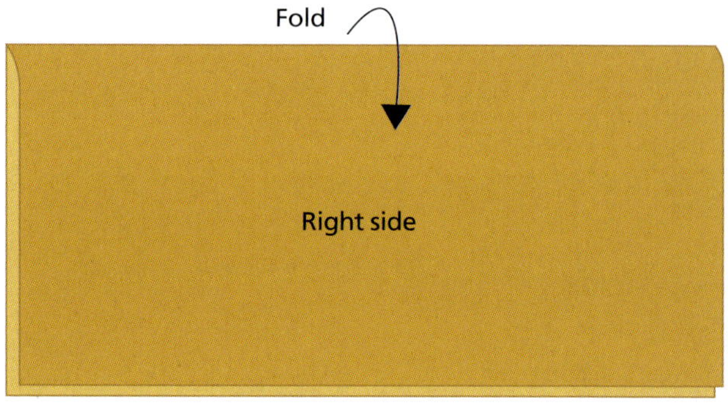

Figure 4

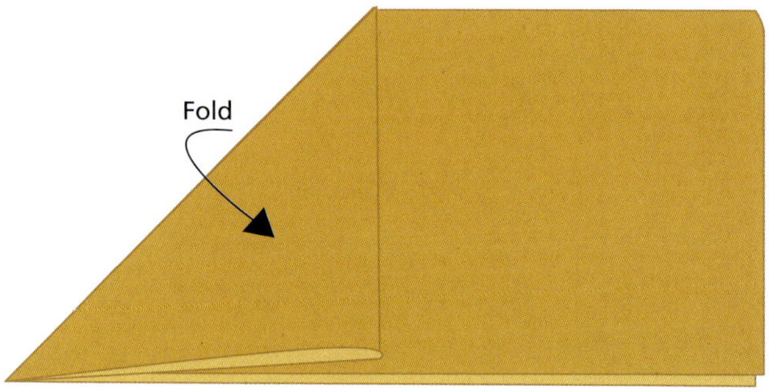

Figure 5

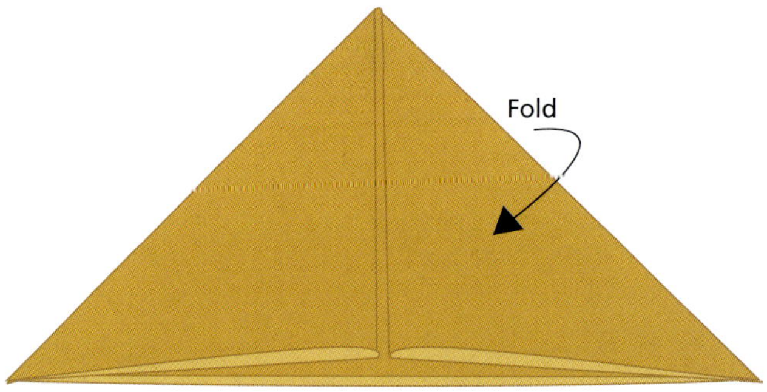

Figure 6

- Column 5: Center and pin 2" (5.1cm) prairie points *facing up* on the background strip, as shown.
  - Insert 2 Fabric A (red) prairie points.
  - Insert 7 Fabric D (medium green print) prairie points.
  - Insert 2 Fabric A (red) prairie points.
  - Insert 3 Fabric B (gold) prairie points.
  - Insert 1 Fabric A (red) prairie point. Figure 11.
- Column 6: Center and pin 5" (12.7cm) prairie points *facing down* on the background strip, as shown.
  - Insert 3 Fabric F (gold print) prairie points.
  - Insert 3 Fabric E (multicolor green) prairie points.
  - Insert 1 Fabric A (red) prairie point. Figure 12.
- Column 7: Center and pin 3" (7.6cm) prairie points *facing down* on the background strip, as shown.
  - Insert 4 Fabric D (medium green print) prairie points.
  - Insert 3 Fabric A (red) prairie points.
  - Insert 1 Fabric C (green) prairie point.
  - Insert 2 Fabric B (gold) prairie points.
  - Insert 1 Fabric C (green) prairie point. Figure 13.

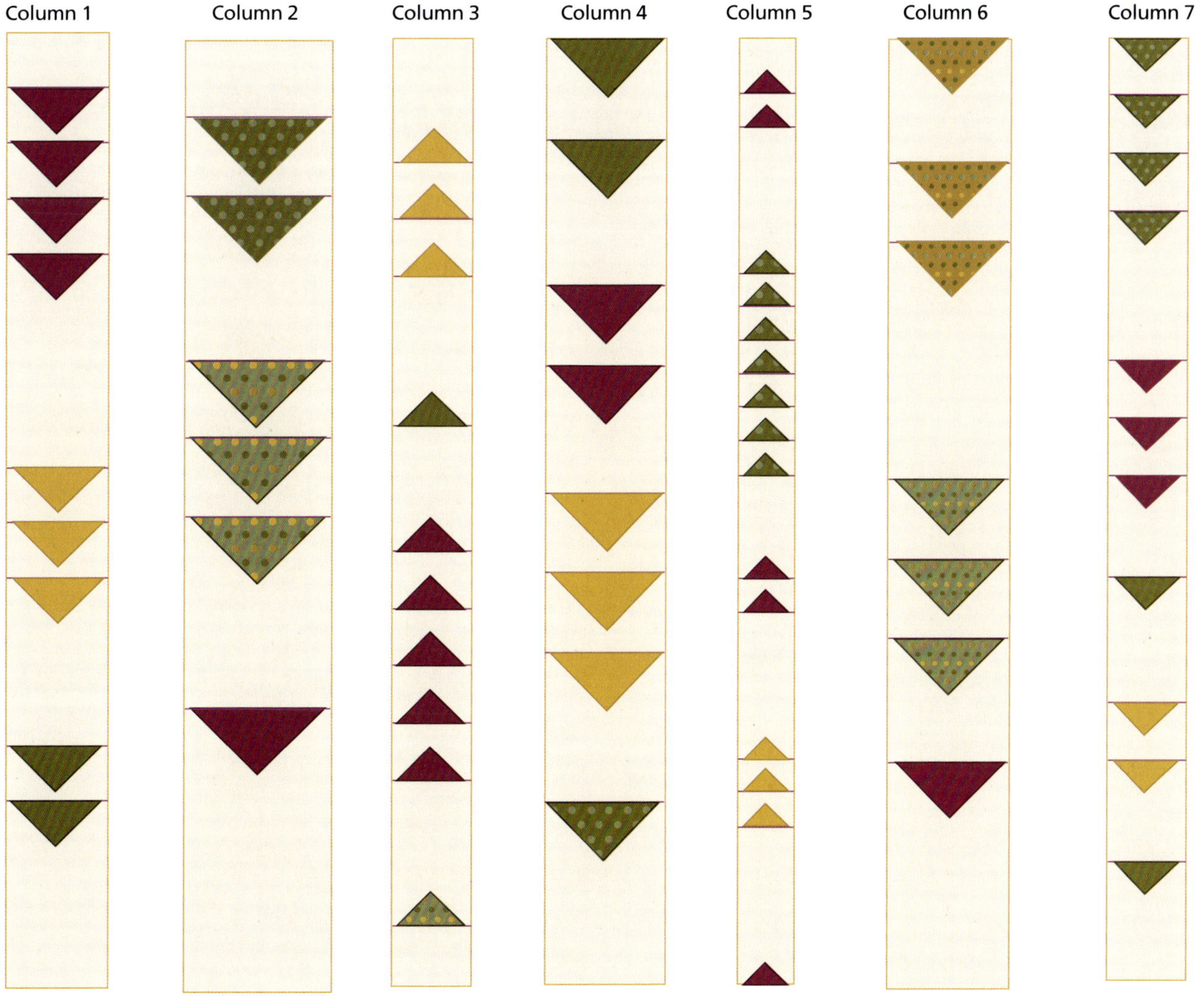

Figure 7 **Figure 8** **Figure 9** **Figure 10** **Figure 11** **Figure 12** **Figure 13**

6 STITCH THE PRAIRIE POINTS TO THE COLUMN BACKGROUND STRIPS

- For best results, assemble 1 column at a time.
- Fold the strip right sides together at each prairie point. The prairie point is sandwiched between the fabric.
- Stitch ¼" (6mm) from the fold.
- Repeat at each prairie point; press the strip. Figure 14.

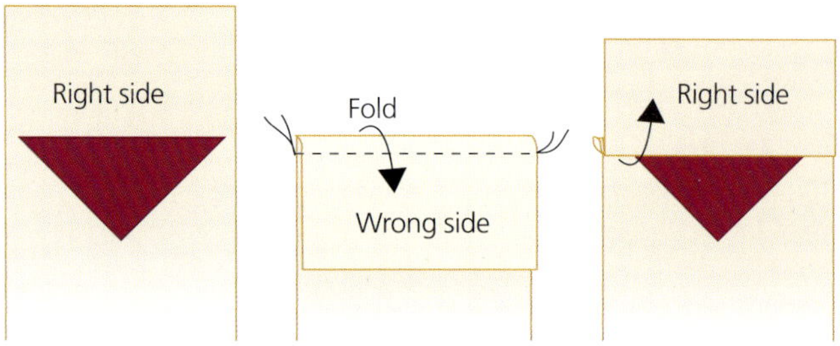

Figure 14

7 ARRANGE AND JOIN COLUMNS FOR THE QUILT

- Using the layout guide (Figure 15), join Columns 1–7 to finish the center of the wall hanging.
- Press seams flat, then to one side.
- Stitch down the center of the folded prairie points with clear monofilament thread to secure. Figure 16.

Figure 15

8 ADD INNER BORDERS

- Measure the sides of the wall hanging.
- Cut two 1"-wide (2.5cm) Fabric G (green) inner borders the length measured.
- Join the borders to the sides of the wall hanging and press seams toward the border.
- Measure the new width of the wall hanging.
- Cut two 1"-wide (2.5cm) Fabric G (green) borders the width measured.

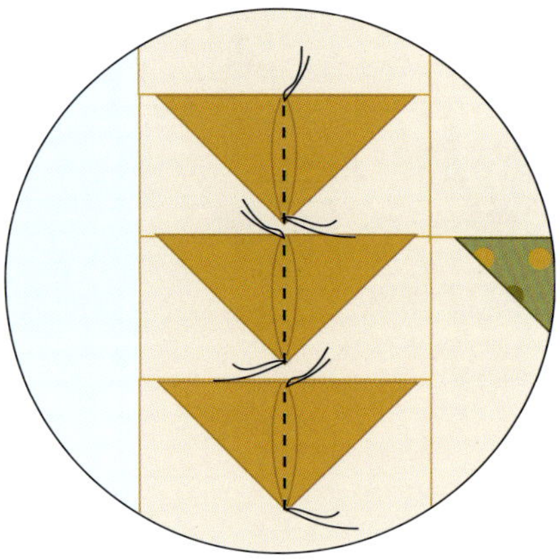

Figure 16

- Join the borders to the top and bottom edges of the wall hanging. Press seams toward the border. Figure 17.
- Repeat the process for the 3" (7.6cm) Fabric H (tan) outer borders. Press seams toward the inner borders. Figure 18.

9 LAYER, QUILT AND BIND

- Complete the wall hanging by layering backing, batting and the wall hanging top. Quilt the layers. Add a rod pocket and add binding, as shown in the basic instructions on pages 114–121.

Figure 17

Figure 18

42" × 44" (106.7cm × 111.8cm)

CHAPTER SIX

Folded Scrappy Column Quilt

Fabric scraps—we all have them, and we often wonder why we're saving them! This quilt, designed as a tummy-time quilt for babies, is the perfect project to use up those treasured scraps. The quilt offers texture—fabric folded in geometric shapes—and plenty of bright color. The next time you need a gift for a newborn, head for your scraps and start cutting and folding.

FINISHED SIZE

- Approximately 42" × 44" (106.7cm × 111.8cm)

SUPPLIES

- Use your personal stash for base and folded fabrics.
- 1 yard (.9m) cotton fabric for narrow column accents and binding
- 1¼ yards (1.1m) backing fabric
- 1¼ yards (1.1m) batting or polyester fleece at least 42" wide (106.7cm)
- Essential Quilting Tools (see listing on page 110)

Note: Because the number, arrangement and positioning of the folded accents and base strips are determined by you, it's impossible to indicate precise yardage for the scraps.

Note: All seam allowances are ¼" (6mm) unless otherwise stated.

1 SELECT, ORGANIZE, PREPARE AND CUT FABRICS

- Choose an assortment of fabric colors.
- Stabilize all fabrics well using spray starch or a starch alternative, such as Mary Ellen's Best Press. See page 112.
- Cut five 2" (5.1cm) crosswise strips of cotton fabric for narrow accent columns. Set aside.
- Cut six 2½" (6.4cm) crosswise strips for the binding. Set aside.
- Cut fabrics for the base strips. Cut 3" (7.6cm) and 4" (10.2cm) crosswise base strips. Then, organize all strips of 1 size within a stack. Figure 1.
- Strip length doesn't matter, but if strips are longer than 22" (55.9cm), cut them in half.
- Cut fabrics for the folded accents. To do this, use small scraps to cut 3" (7.6cm) and 4" (10.2cm) squares or rectangles, with the strip width as 1 of the dimensions. Figure 2.
- From small scraps, cut 2" (5.1cm) squares to be used as dimension accents for the narrow column accent strips, which separate the design strips.

NOTE FROM NANCY

As mentioned, the featured quilt has 3" (7.6cm) and 4" (10.2cm) base strips. You're not limited to those widths. You could easily cut the base strips and folded accent strips wider, 5"–6" (12.7cm–15.2cm). The choice is yours.

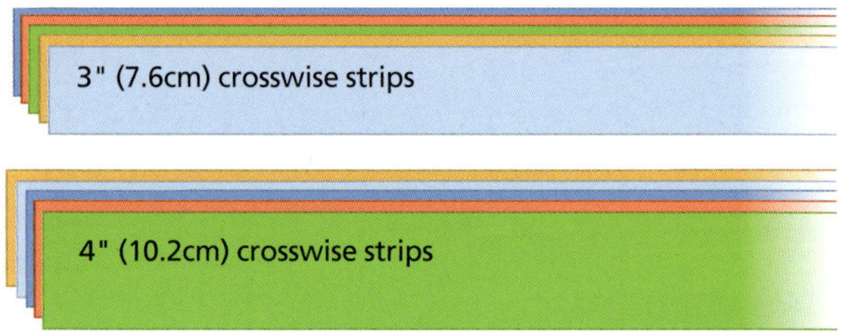

Figure 1

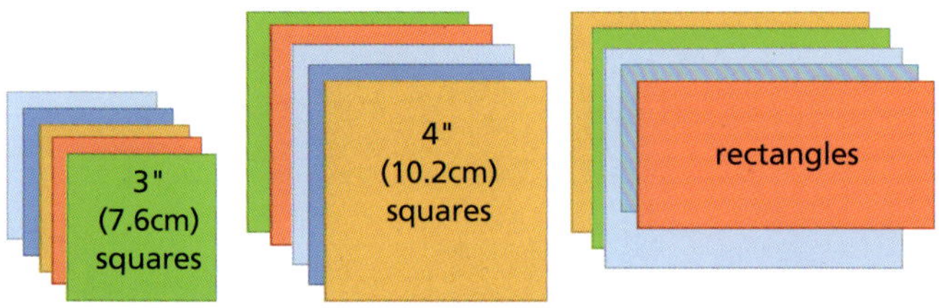

Figure 2

2 PREPARE THE FOLDED ACCENTS

Use pressing, rather than sewing, to prepare these accents. Be creative. Here are a few ideas to get you started.

- Folded rectangles
  - Fold the fabric in half, wrong sides together. Figure 3.
- Trapezoids
  - Fold a square or rectangle in half, wrong sides together. Press.
  - Meet one folded corner to the cut edge. Press. Figure 4.
- Prairie points
  - Fold a square in half, wrong sides together.
  - Meet one corner of the folded edge to the cut edge and form a point. Press.
  - Repeat with the second corner fold. Doing so will form a triangular section with folds that meet at the center. Figure 5.

Note: The side of the prairie point that has the fold can be visible, or you can place the fold face down on the quilt.

- Folded right triangles
  - Fold a square in half, corner to corner, wrong sides together.
  - Press the folded edge. Since the edge is bias, it will stretch. Be careful to avoid distorting the edge. Figure 6.
- Folded triangle variation 1
  - Create a folded right triangle. Bring one point to the 90° corner. Press. Figure 7.

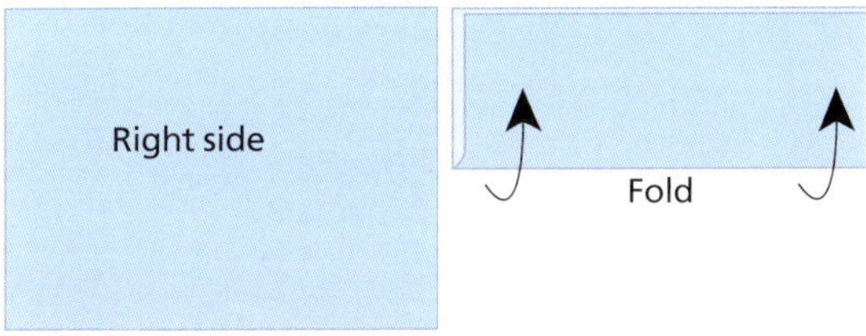

Figure 3

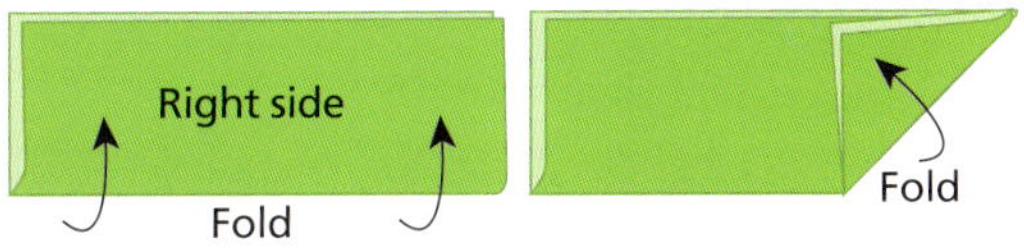

Figure 4

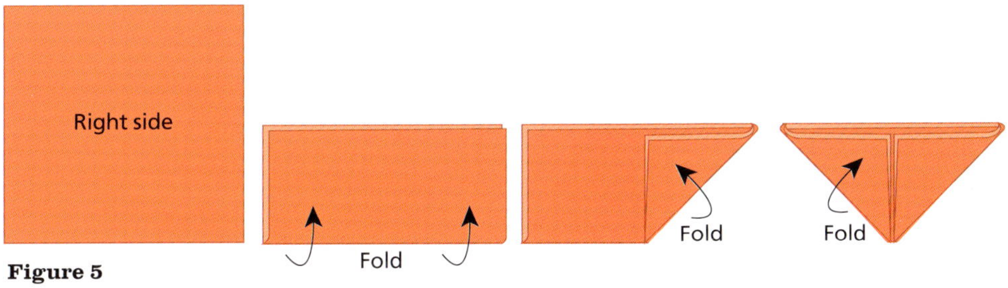

Figure 5

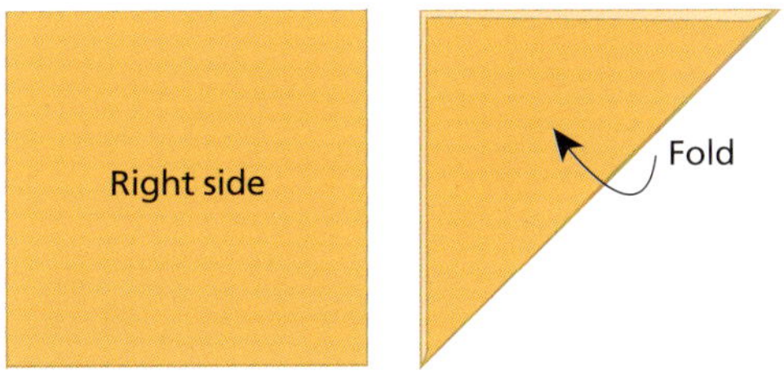

Figure 6

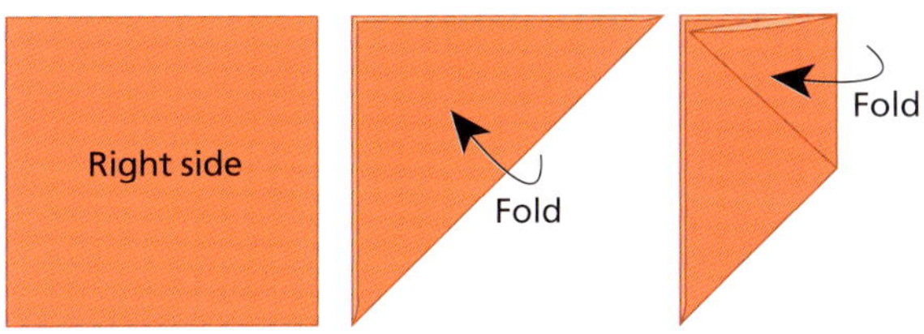

Figure 7

NOTE FROM NANCY

Consider including other types of fabrics for added texture. Babies enjoy touching and feeling fabrics that are napped, satiny and have surface texture. Just be aware that if the quilt will be laundered, fabrics should also be washable.

- Folded triangle variation 2
  - Create a folded right triangle. Bring both points to the 90° corner. Press. Figure 8.
- Press fabrics to give them a crisp edge before adding them to the design.
- Prepare stacks of quilt elements, then lay out a design. Move the accents around until you like the design.

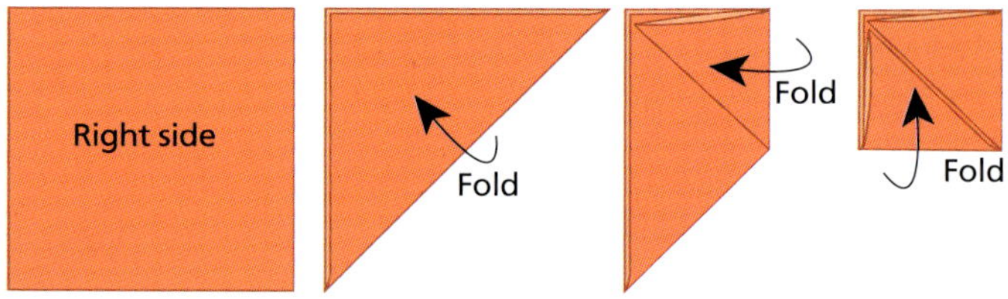

Figure 8

3 SET UP THE MACHINE FOR STITCHING

- Attach a patchwork foot and insert a quilting needle.
- Thread both the top of the machine and the bobbin with all-purpose thread.

Note: Remember to clean the machine after each use. Lint accumulates in the feed dog area, especially if you work with napped or textured fabrics.

4 PREPARE THE BASE COLUMNS

Select 2 strips of the same width. Join strips and add a folded accent where the 2 strips meet. Select an accent that contrasts with the base strips in color or design so it will complement the design rather than blend in with the base.

- Position the folded accent on the short edge of 1 of the strips, right sides together and cut edges matched. Figure 9.
- Add the second strip, again meeting right sides. Figure 10.
- Join strips with a ¼" (6mm) seam. Figure 11.
- Position and stitch a second set of strips and once again include a folded accent. Continue to chain stitch sets of strips with folded accents.
- After joining multiple strips, separate them by cutting the chain stitching between strips.
- As an option to the folded accents shown, you can add folded accents within a strip. To do this, fold the strip, right sides together and meet lengthwise cut edges. Press the fold. Figure 12.

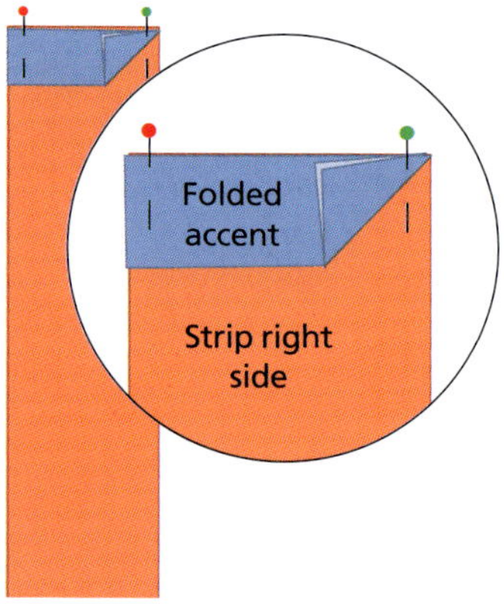

Figure 9

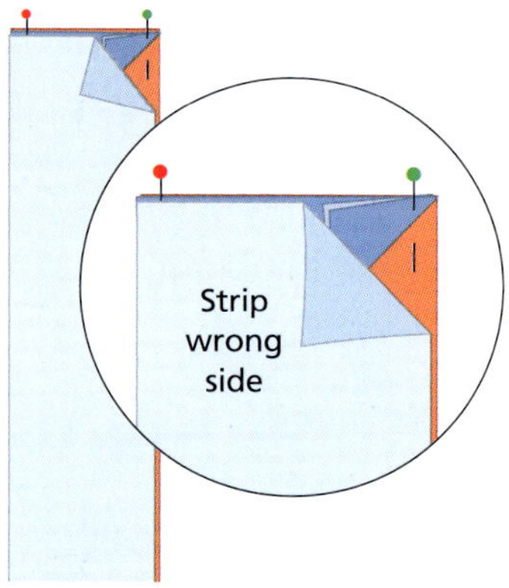

Figure 10

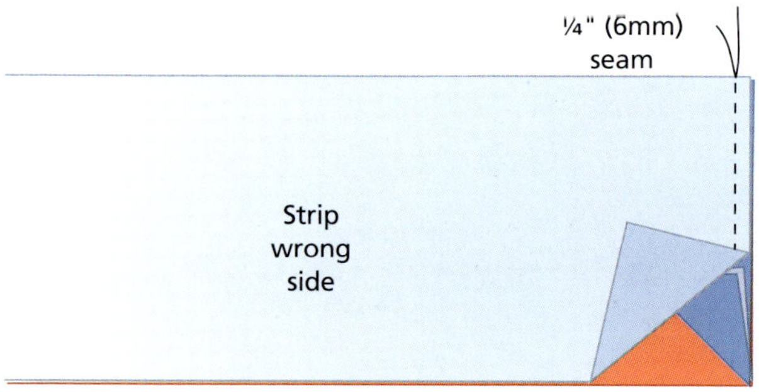

Figure 11

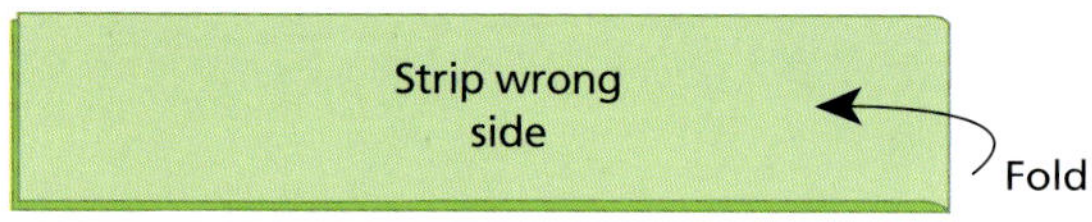

Figure 12

- Unfold the strip; position the cut edges of a folded accent along the pressed line. Figure 13.
- Refold the strip and stitch ¼" (6mm) from the folded edge. Figure 14.
- Unfold the strip and press.
- Join strips to make columns the desired length.
- Prepare the number of columns needed for the quilt. Press seams flat, then to 1 side.

5 ADD NARROW COLUMN ACCENT STRIPS

These strips help visually break up the design to make the dimensional columns more predominant.

- Join 2" (5.1cm) narrow column accent strips as needed to equal the length of the columns.
- Join narrow column accent strips to both edges of the first column, right sides together. Press seams toward the narrow column accent strips. Figure 15.
- Join narrow column accent strips to only the right edge of the remaining columns.
- Join the remaining columns to finish the quilt top.

6 LAYER, QUILT AND BIND

- Use your favorite methods or refer to pages 114–121.
- Use the binding strips for the binding.

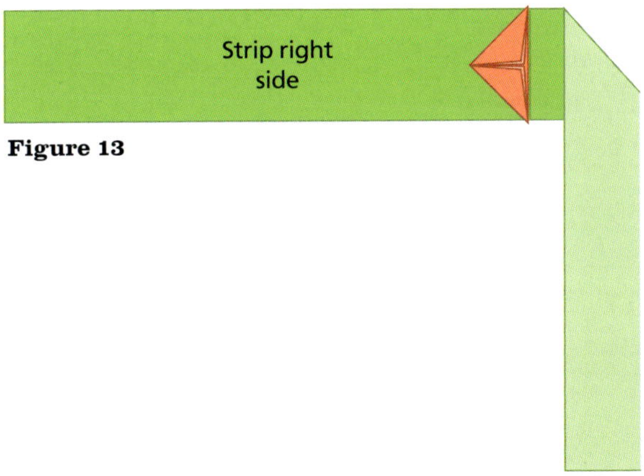

Figure 13

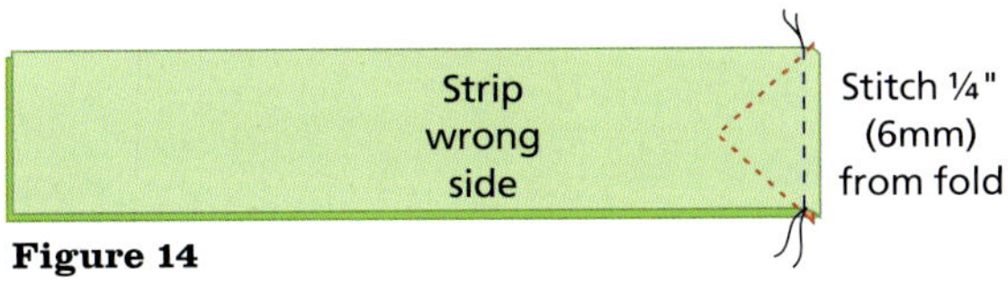

Figure 14

Figure 15

16½" × 21½" (41.9cm × 54.6cm)

CHAPTER SEVEN

Dotted Columns Wall Hanging

Switch it up by making an abstract wall hanging with column-quilt techniques and fun fabrics. This artistic silk dupioni wall hanging includes "dotted columns"—circles appliquéd over the easy-to-create columns. Use a tool designed especially for making circles, such as the Circles Sew Simple Tool—it makes the circles fast, painlessly and perfect!

FINISHED SIZE

- Approximately 16½" × 21½" (41.9cm × 54.6cm)

SUPPLIES

- Fat eighths (9" × 21"[22.9cm × 53.3cm]) Fabrics A–E for large columns
- ¼ yard (.2m) Fabric F (taupe) for scrappy binding and narrow columns
- ⅛ yard (.1m) Fabric G (white) for scrappy binding and narrow columns
- Fat eighths (9" × 21" [22.9cm × 53.3cm]) Fabrics H–J for appliqué circles
- ½ yard (.5m) lightweight fusible interfacing
- ½ yard (.5m) batting
- ½ yard (.5m) backing fabric
- Sewer's Fix-It tape or masking tape
- Circles Sew Simple Tool (optional)
- Essential Quilting Tools (see listing on page 110)

Note: All seam allowances are ¼" (6mm) unless otherwise stated.

1 PREPARE AND CUT FABRICS

- Stabilize all fabrics well using spray starch or a starch alternative, such as Mary Ellen's Best Press. See page 112.
- Fabric A (yellow-green) for large columns:
  - Cut one 2½" × 21" (6.4cm x 53.3cm) strip. Subcut this strip into one 2½" × 8½" (6.4cm × 21.6cm) rectangle, one 2½" × 3½" (6.4cm × 8.9cm) rectangle and one 2½" × 4½" (6.4cm × 11.4cm) rectangle.
  - Cut one 4½" (11.4cm) square.
  - Cut one 3½" × 6½" (8.9cm × 16.5cm) rectangle. Figure 1.
- Fabric B (dark yellow-green) for large columns:
  - Cut one 3½" × 7½" (8.9cm × 19.1cm) rectangle. Figure 2.
- Fabric C (dark olive) for large columns:
  - Cut one 2½" × 21" (6.4cm × 53.3cm) strip.
  - Subcut this strip into one 2½" × 3½" (6.4cm × 8.9cm) rectangle and one 2½" × 9½" (6.4cm × 24.1cm) rectangle.
  - Cut one 4½" × 21" (11.4cm × 53.3cm) strip. Subcut this strip into one 4½" × 3½" (8.9cm × 11.4cm) rectangle and one 4½" × 5½" (11.4cm × 14.0cm) rectangle.

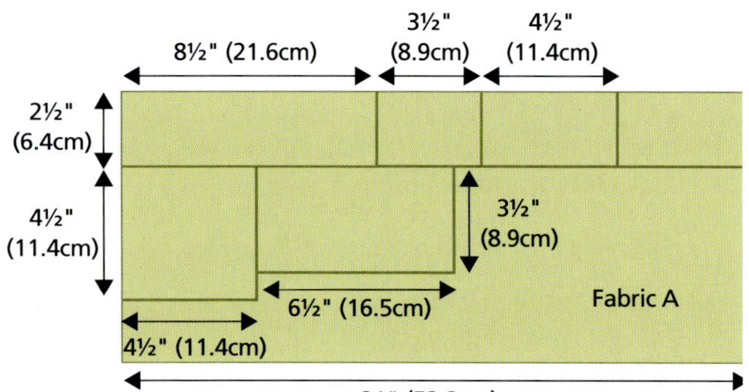

Figure 1

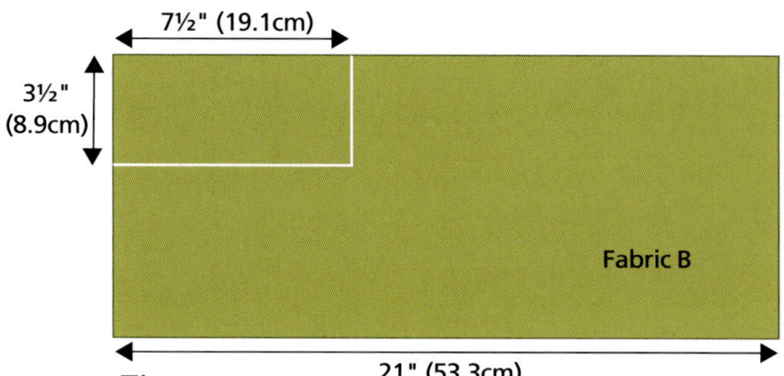

Figure 2

- Cut one 3½" (8.9cm) square. Figure 3.

- Fabric D (medium yellow-green) for large columns:
  - Cut one 2½" × 8½" (6.4cm × 21.6cm) rectangle and one 3½" × 10½" (8.9cm × 26.7cm) rectangle. Figure 4.
- Fabric E (sage) for large columns:
  - Cut one 2½" × 21" (6.4cm x 53.3cm) strip.
  - Subcut the strip into one 2½" × 5½" (6.4cm × 14.0cm) rectangle and one 2½" × 3½" (6.4cm x 8.9cm) rectangle. Figure 5.
- Fabric F (taupe):
  - Cut two 1½" (3.8cm) crosswise strips for narrow columns.
  - Subcut the strip into one 1½" × 3½" (3.8cm × 8.9cm) rectangle, one 1½" × 5½" (3.8cm × 14.0cm) rectangle, two 1½" × 6½" (3.8cm x 16.5cm) rectangles, one 1½" × 9½" (3.8cm × 24.1cm) rectangle, one 1½" × 10½" (3.8cm × 26.7cm) rectangle and one 1½" (3.8cm) square for the narrow columns.
  - Cut three 1½" (3.8cm) crosswise strips for binding; set aside. Figure 6.
- Fabric G (white):
  - Cut two 1½" (3.8cm) crosswise strips for narrow columns.
  - Subcut the strip into one 1½" × 2½" (3.8cm × 6.4cm) rectangle, one 1½" × 3½" (3.8cm × 8.9cm) rectangle, one 1½" × 4½" (3.8cm x 11.4cm) rectangle, two 1½" × 5½" (3.8cm × 14cm) rectangles, one 1½" × 6½" (3.8cm × 16.5cm) rectangle, one 1½" × 7½" (3.8cm × 19.1cm) rectangle and one 1½" × 8½" (3.8cm × 21.6cm) rectangle for the narrow columns.
  - Cut one 1½" (3.8cm) crosswise strip for the binding; set aside. Figure 7.
- Batting and backing: Subcut batting and backing into 18" × 24" (45.7cm × 61cm) rectangles.

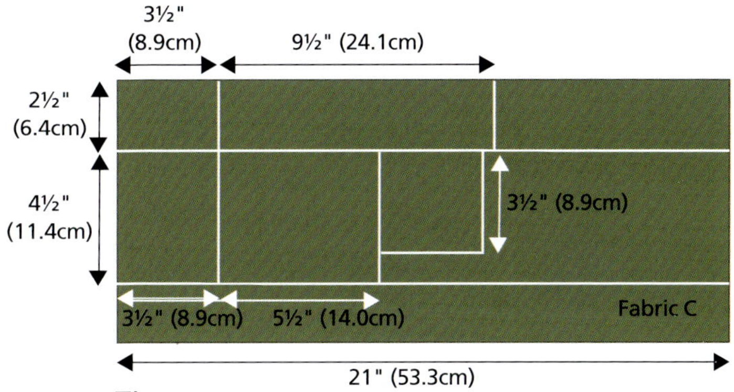

Figure 3

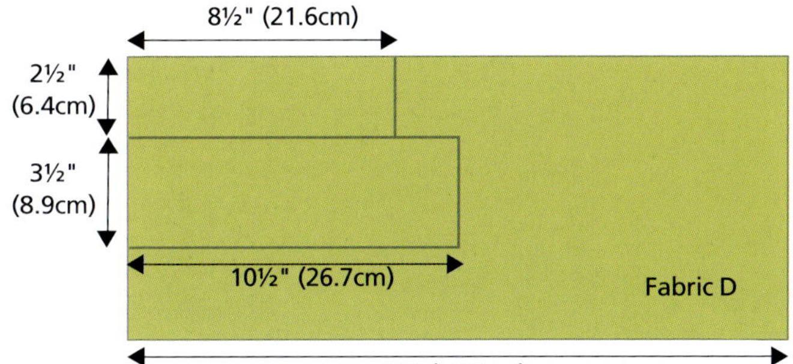

Figure 4

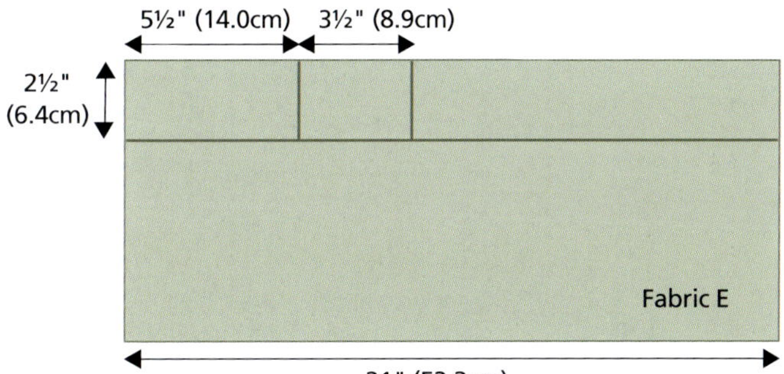

Figure 5

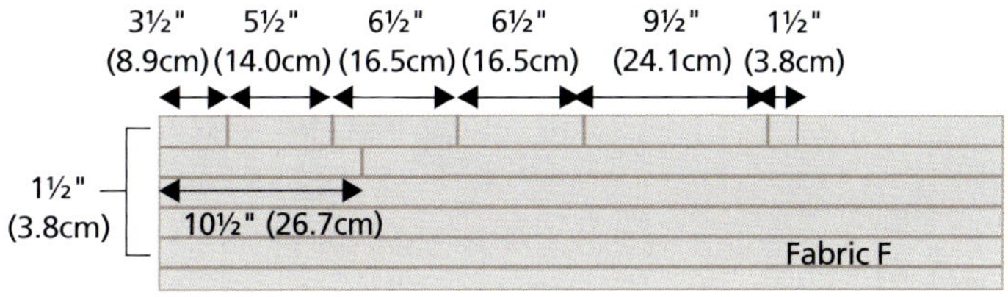

Figure 6

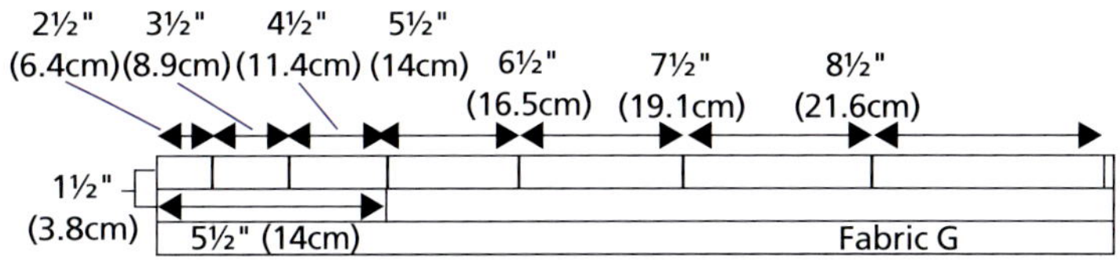

Figure 7

2 PREPARE APPLIQUÉ FABRICS

- Fuse interfacing to the wrong side of Fabric H (magenta), Fabric I (orange) and Fabric J (turquoise) for appliqué circles. Figure 8.

3 ARRANGE AND JOIN CUT SECTIONS TO COMPLETE EACH COLUMN

Press the seams toward darker fabrics.

- Column 1:
  - Join a short end of a 3½" × 6½" (8.9cm × 16.5cm) Fabric A (yellow-green) rectangle to a short end of a 3½" × 7½" (8.9cm × 19.1cm) Fabric B (dark yellow-green) rectangle, right sides together.
  - Join a short end of a 3½" (8.9cm) square of Fabric C (dark olive) to the remaining short end of the Fabric B (dark yellow-green) rectangle, right sides together to complete Column 1. Figure 9.
- Column 2:
  - Join a short end of a 1½" × 10½" (3.8cm × 26.7cm) Fabric F (taupe) rectangle to a short end of a 1½" × 3½" (3.8cm × 8.9cm) the Fabric G (white) rectangle, right sides together.
  - Join a short end of a 1½" × 3½" (3.8cm × 8.9cm) Fabric F (taupe) rectangle to the remaining short end of Fabric G (white) rectangle, right sides together, to complete Column 2. Figure 10.
- Column 3:
  - Join a short end of a 2½" × 8½" (6.4cm × 21.6cm) Fabric D (medium yellow-green) rectangle to a short end of a 2½" × 3½" (6.4cm × 8.9cm) Fabric C (dark olive) rectangle, right sides together.
  - Join a short end of a 2½" × 5½" (6.4cm × 14.0cm) Fabric E (sage) rectangle to the remaining short end of the Fabric C (dark olive) rectangle, right sides together, to complete Column 3. Figure 11.
- Column 4:
  - Join a short end of a 1½" × 6½" (3.8cm × 16.5cm) Fabric G (white) rectangle to a short end of a 1½" × 6½" (3.8cm × 16.5cm) Fabric F (taupe) rectangle, right sides together.

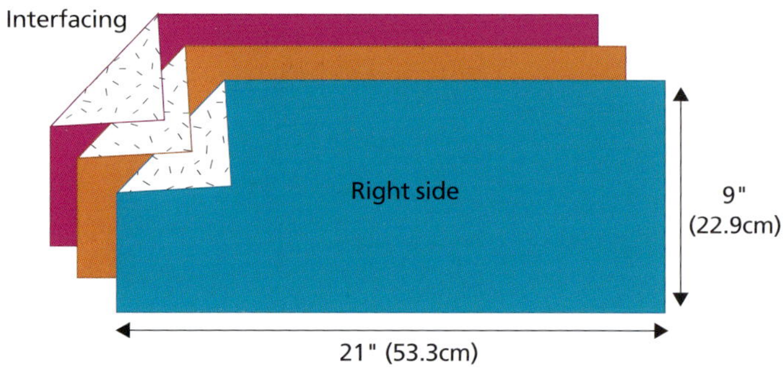

Figure 8

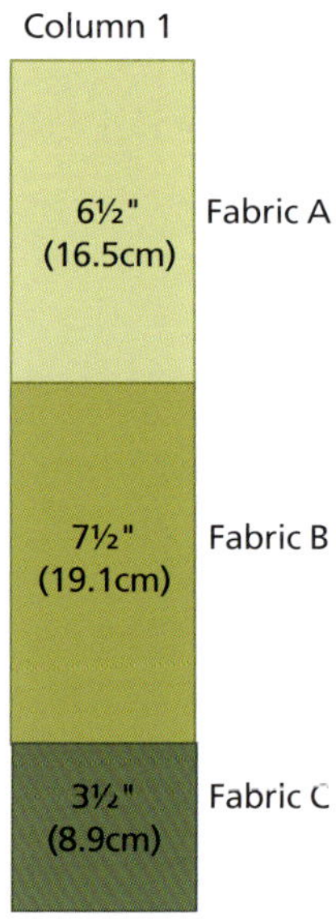

Figure 9

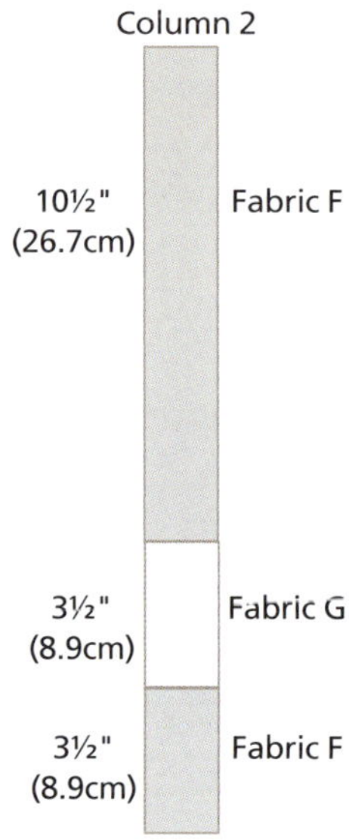

Figure 10

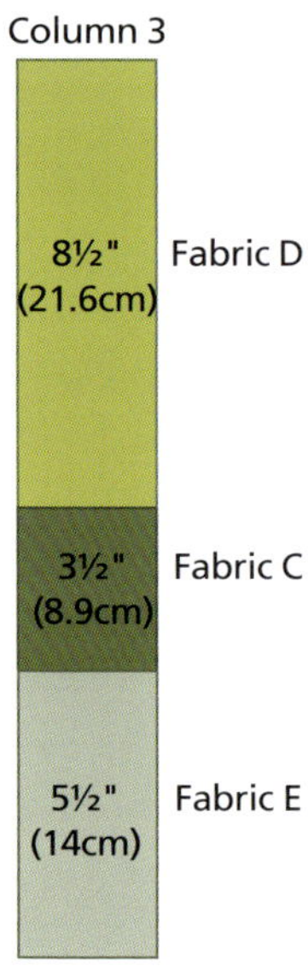

Figure 11

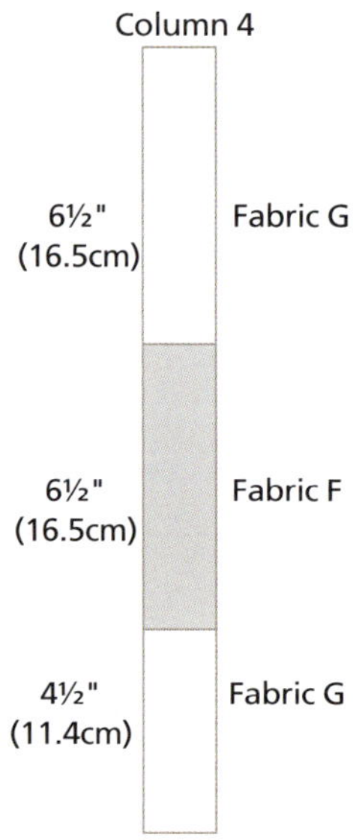

Figure 12

- Join a short end of a 1½" × 4½" (3.8cm × 11.4cm) Fabric G (white) rectangle to the remaining short end of the Fabric F (taupe) rectangle, right sides together, to complete Column 4. Figure 12.

- Column 5:
  - Join a short end of a 4½" × 5½" (11.4cm × 14cm) Fabric C (dark olive) rectangle to a 4½" (11.4cm) Fabric A (yellow green) square, right sides together.
  - Join a short end of a 4½" × 7½" (11.4cm × 19.1cm) Fabric B (dark yellow-green) rectangle to the Fabric A (yellow-green) square, right sides together, to complete Column 5. Figure 13.
- Column 6:
  - Join a short end of a 1½" × 7½" (3.8cm × 19.1cm) Fabric G (white) rectangle to a 1½" (3.8cm) Fabric F (taupe) square, right sides together.
  - Join a short end of a 1½" × 8½" (3.8cm × 21.6cm) Fabric G (white) rectangle to the Fabric F (taupe) square, right sides together, to complete Column 6. Figure 14.
- Column 7:
  - Join a short end of a 2½" × 6½" (6.4cm × 16.5cm) Fabric B (dark yellow-green) rectangle to a short end of a 2½" × 8½" (6.4cm x 21.6cm) Fabric A (yellow-green) rectangle, right sides together.
  - Join a 2½" (6.4cm) Fabric B (dark yellow-green) square to the remaining short end of Fabric A (yellow-green) rectangle, right sides together, to complete Column 7. Figure 15.
- Column 8:
  - Join a short end of a 1½" × 5½" (3.8cm × 14.0cm) Fabric G (white) rectangle to a short end of a 1½" × 6½" (3.8cm × 16.5cm) Fabric F (taupe) rectangle, right sides together.
  - Join a 1½" × 5½" (3.8cm × 14.0cm) Fabric G (white) rectangle to the remaining short end of Fabric F (taupe) rectangle, right sides together, to complete Column 8. Figure 16.

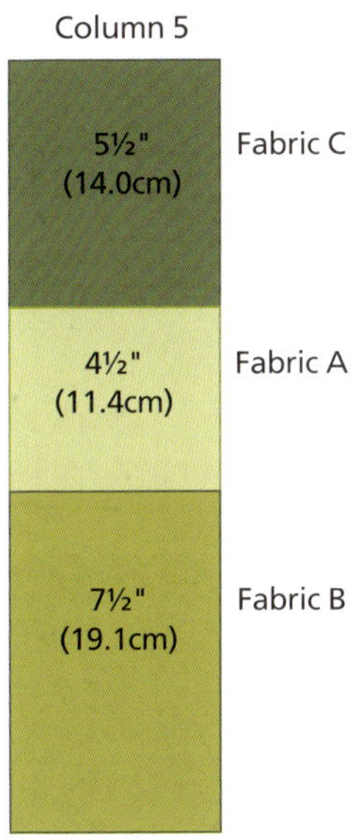

Figure 13

Figure 14

Figure 15

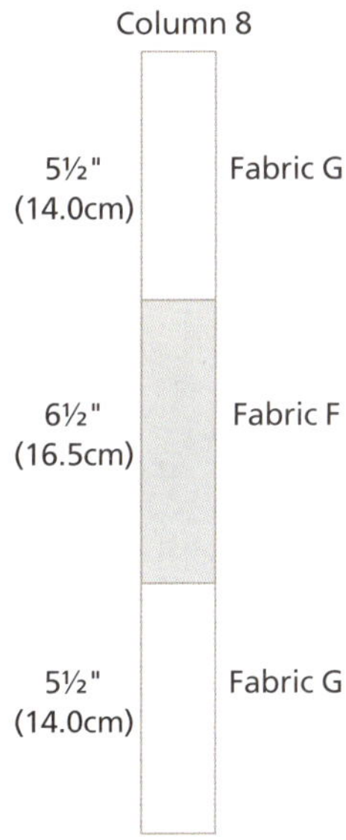

Figure 16

- Column 9:
  - Join a short end of a 2½" × 3½" (6.4cm × 8.9cm) Fabric A (yellow-green) rectangle to a short end of a 2½" × 9½" (6.4cm × 24.1cm) Fabric C (dark olive) rectangle, right sides together.
  - Join a 2½" × 4½" (6.4cm × 11.4cm) Fabric A (yellow-green) rectangle to the remaining short end of Fabric C (dark olive) rectangle, right sides together, to complete Column 9. Figure 17.
- Column 10:
  - Join a short end of a 1½" × 5½" (3.8cm × 14.0cm) Fabric F (taupe) rectangle to a short end of a 1½" × 2½" (3.8cm × 6.4cm) Fabric G (white) rectangle, right sides together.
  - Join a 1½" × 9½" (3.8cm × 24.1cm) Fabric F (taupe) rectangle to the remaining short end of the Fabric G (white) rectangle, right sides together, to complete Column 10. Figure 18.
- Column 11:
  - Join a short end of a 3½" × 4½" (8.9cm × 11.4cm) Fabric C (olive) rectangle to a short end of a 3½" × 10½" (8.9cm × 26.7cm) Fabric D (medium yellow-green) rectangle, right sides together.
  - Join a 3½" × 2½" (8.9cm × 6.4cm) Fabric E (sage) rectangle to the remaining short end of the Fabric D (medium yellow-green) rectangle, right sides together, to complete Column 11. Figure 19.

4 JOIN COLUMNS

- Join Column 1 to 2, 3 to 4, 5 to 6, 7 to 8 and 9 to 10, right sides together. Press seams toward wide columns. Figure 20.
- Join Column 2 to 3, 4 to 5, 6 to 7, 8 to 9 and 10 to 11, right sides together. Press seams toward wide columns.

Figure 17

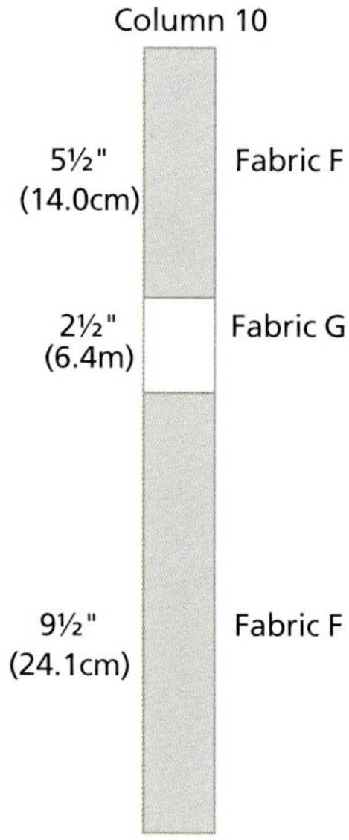

Figure 18

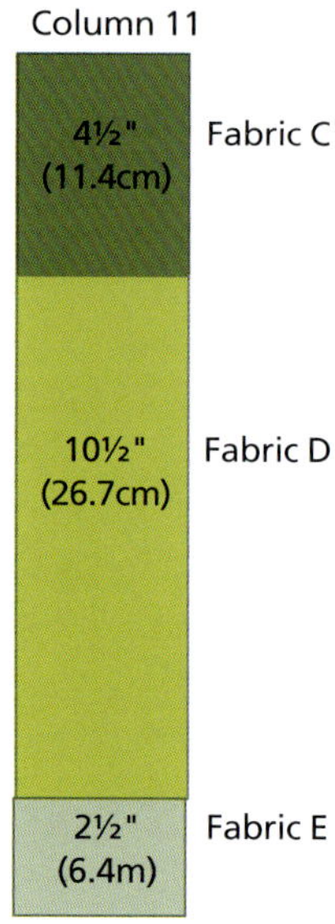

Figure 19

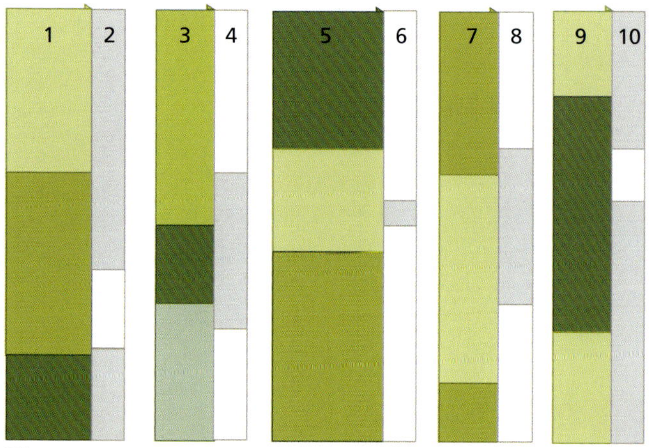

Figure 20

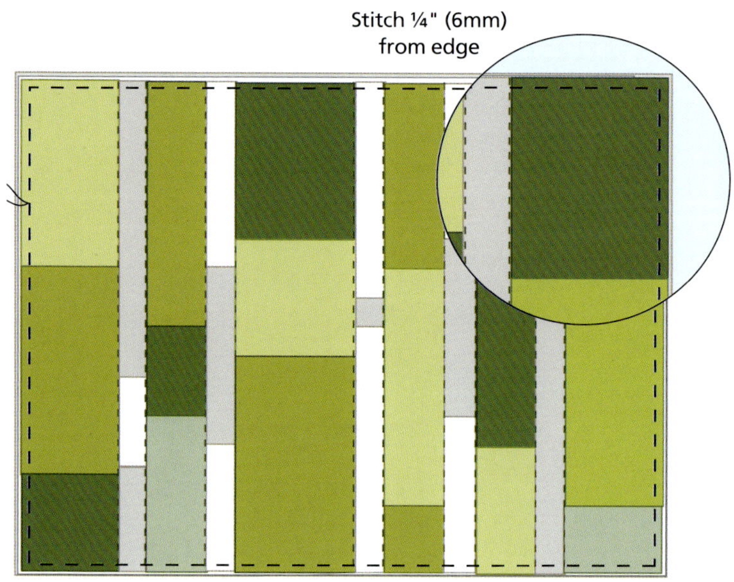

Figure 21

5 LAYER AND QUILT THE WALL HANGING

- Place backing fabric, wrong side up, on a flat surface.
- Securely tape backing to the surface using Sewer's Fix-It Tape or masking tape.
- Position batting over the backing.
- Center the wall hanging, right side up, over batting.
- Pin all layers together using curved basting pins, starting in the center of the fabric and working toward the outer edges.
- Remove tape when pinning is complete.
- Stitch in the ditch of each column seam, removing pins as you come to them. See basic techniques on page 117.
- Baste ¼" (6mm) from the edges of the wall hanging through all layers; trim excess batting and backing. Figure 21.

6 CREATE CIRCLE APPLIQUÉS

- Attach the Circles Sew Simple Tool to the bed of the sewing machine.
- Thread the machine with coordinating thread for both top and bobbin to match the appliqué.
- Mark the center pivot point of each circle on the quilted wall hanging. Figure 22.
- Set the Circles Sew Simple Tool for a 4" (10.2cm) circle.
- Cut a fabric square 2"–3" (5.1cm–7.6cm) larger than the size of the completed appliqué.
- Position the quilted wall hanging over the tack portion of the tool, and align the center pivot point of the size 4" (10.2cm) circle.
- Position the appliqué fabric square over the tack and secure the tack with the guard that comes with the tool.
- Straight stitch the circle, then trim excess fabric close to the straight stitching line. Figure 23.
- Set the machine for a satin stitch (wide zigzag and short stitch length) and stitch again over the 4" (10.2cm) straight stitched circle. Figure 24.
- Repeat for all of the circle sizes.

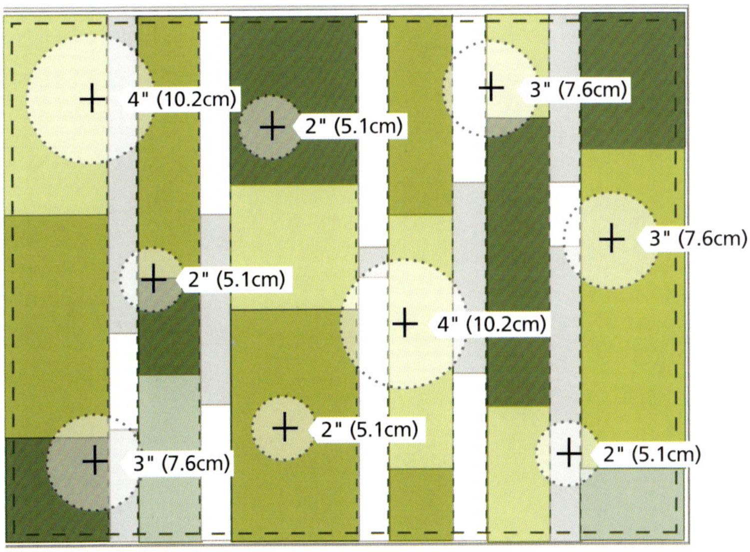

Figure 22

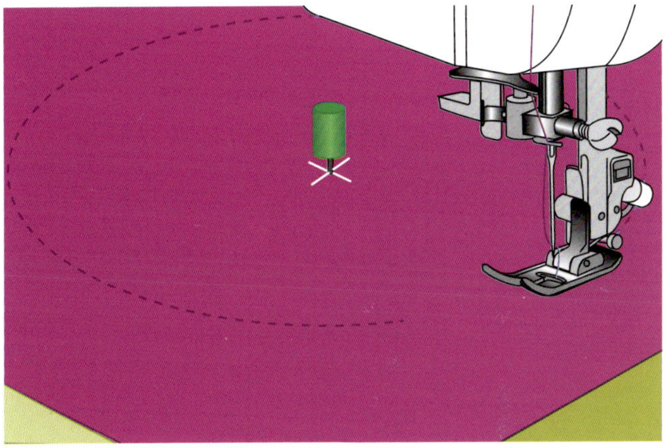

Figure 23

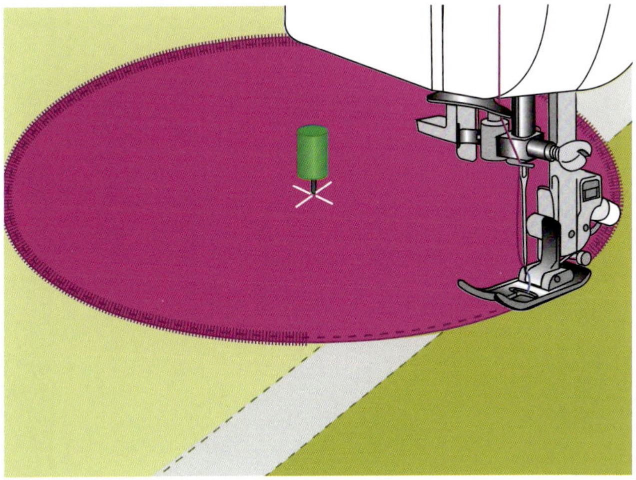

Figure 24

7 CREATE A SCRAPPY BINDING

- Alternate and join the short ends of the 1½" (3.8cm) subcut strips of Fabric F and Fabric G, right sides together. Press seams toward dark fabrics. Figure 25.
- Join the 2 remaining 1½" (3.8cm) strips of Fabric F, right sides together, with a diagonal seam. Press seam open. Figure 26.
- Join the lengthwise edges of the scrappy strip to the solid strip, right sides together. Press the lengthwise seam flat, then open. Figure 27.
- Fold the pieced binding strip, wrong sides together with the lengthwise raw edges meeting. Press along the seam edge to create the scrappy binding. One side of the binding is solid, and the other side is scrappy. Figure 28.

Figure 25

Figure 26

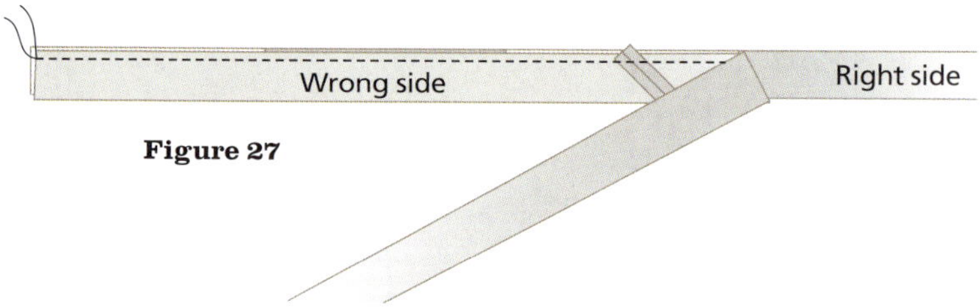

Figure 27

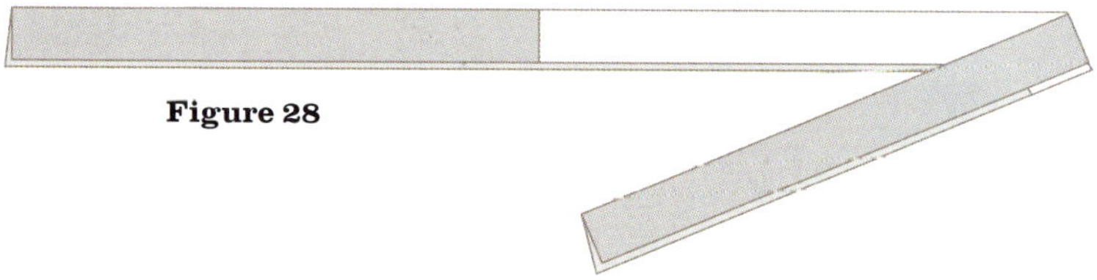

Figure 28

8 ATTACH SCRAPPY BINDING

- Place the scrappy side of the binding on the right side of the wall hanging.
- Optional: Add a rod pocket using your favorite technique or see the instructions on page 119.
- Attach binding to wall hanging using your favorite binding technique, or see instructions on pages 120–121. Figure 29.

Figure 29

NOTE FROM NANCY

If you don't have a Sew Circles Simple Tool, trace circular shapes—bases of cups or drinking glasses—on squares of fabric which will be used for the circle appliqués. Pin the appliqué fabric to the quilt top. Straight stitch around the circle and trim off the excess fabric as detailed on page 51. Then, satin stitch around the circular shape.

CREATIVE OPTIONS

Primary colors in cotton fabrics give this mini-column quilt a totally different look.

80" × 88" (203.2cm × 223.5cm)

CHAPTER EIGHT

Happy-Go-Lucky Chevron Column Quilt

Use novel piecing techniques in this *Happy-Go-Lucky Chevron Column Quilt*. Mix and match the wide and narrow strips of fabric to create carefree chevron columns. No matching necessary—and use only straight stitching!

FINISHED SIZE

- Approximately 80" × 88" (203.2cm × 223.5cm) full/double-size quilt

SUPPLIES

- 3⅓ yards (3.1m) print fabric
- ¾–1 yard (.7m–.9m) each of 6 to 8 solid fabrics
- Approximately 2¼ yards (2.1m) backing fabric 108"-wide (274.3cm)
- Full-size batting (81" × 96" [205.7cm × 243.8cm])
- Large cutting mat: 24" × 36" (61cm × 91.4cm) or larger
- Two 6" × 24" (15.2cm × 61cm) rulers
- Permanent marker or masking tape
- Essential Quilting Tools (see listing on page 110)

NOTE FROM NANCY

Choose the print fabric first, then find solids that match or coordinate. Some of the fabrics used for this quilt measured less than a yard; others measured over a yard. Design it as you go for a unique look! You might choose 6, 7 or 8 fabrics; it's up to you.

Note: All seam allowances are ¼" (6mm) unless otherwise stated.

1 PREPARE AND CUT FABRICS

- Stabilize all fabrics well using spray starch or a starch alternative such as Mary Ellen's Best Press. See page 112.
- Cut thirty-three 6" (15.2cm) crosswise strips of solid fabrics. Use the full width of a standard 6" × 24" (15.2cm × 61.0cm) ruler to quickly measure. Not all of the colors in the featured quilt have the same number of crosswise cuts. Some colors are featured 3, 4 or 5 times. Figure 1.
- Cut forty-seven 2½" (6.4cm) crosswise strips of print fabric.
- Separate the print fabric strips into 2 stacks: 15 for the chevron columns and 32 for the narrow columns, borders and binding.

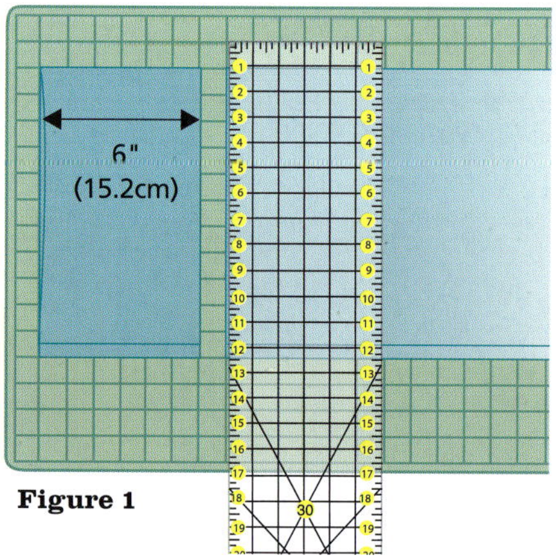

Figure 1

NOTE FROM NANCY

Piece the back similar to the scrappy backing shown on page 114. Use your scraps to give the backing some well-deserved interest! Learn tips for piecing the backing on page 113.

2 ARRANGE FABRICS INTO THREE GROUPINGS

- Divide fabrics into 3 groupings with eleven 6" (15.2cm) solid crosswise strips and five 2½" (6.4cm) print crosswise strips in each grouping. Each grouping will create 2 columns.
- Cut crosswise strips of 1 grouping in half, creating 21" (53.3cm) lengths. There are now 2 groups of 42"-long (106.7cm) strips and 2 groups of 21"-long (53.3cm) strips. Figure 2.

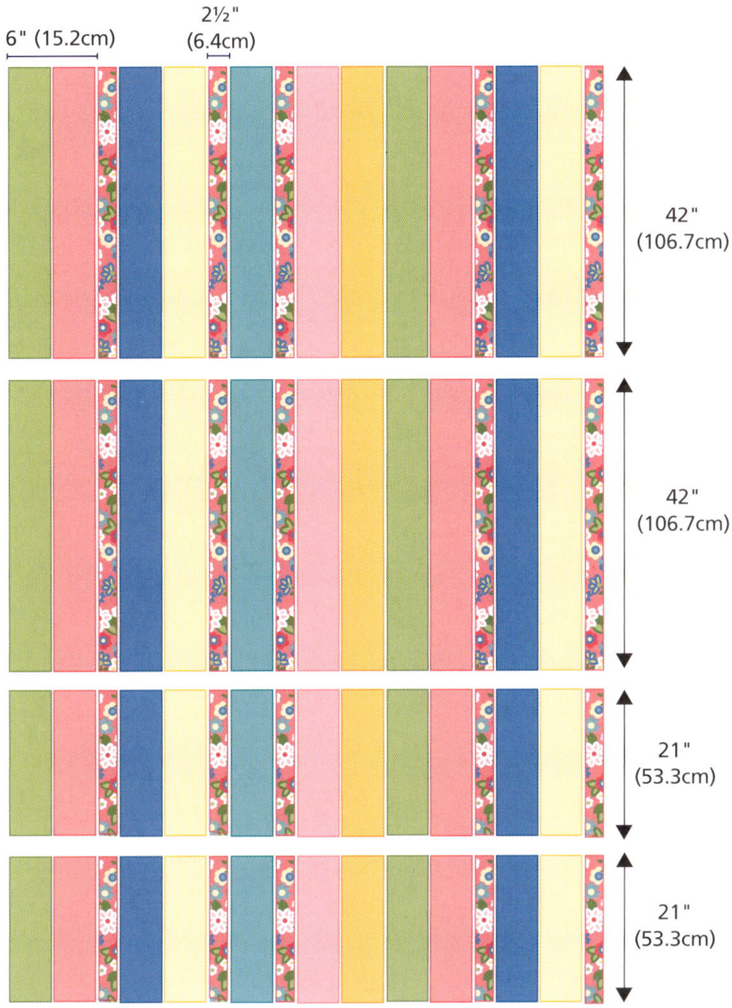

Figure 2

3 STITCH DOWNSTAIRS STRATAS

Downstairs stratas refers to the downward steplike arrangement from left to right.

- Lay out 42" (106.7cm) crosswise strips from 1 grouping, and randomly place the print strips among the solids. (There is no right or wrong arrangement.)
- Rather than sewing all 16 strips (11 solids and 5 prints) together, create 3 subsets of 5 or 6 pieces. Small subsets are easier to handle.
- Fold the upper *right* corner of each strip to the left side, creating a 45° angle. Figure 3.
- Place a pin at the fold, then allow the corner to unfold Repeat for all 16 strips. Figure 4.
- With the right sides together, align 2 strips, with the second strip ¼" (6mm) above the pin. Figure 5.
- Join the long edges. Figure 6.

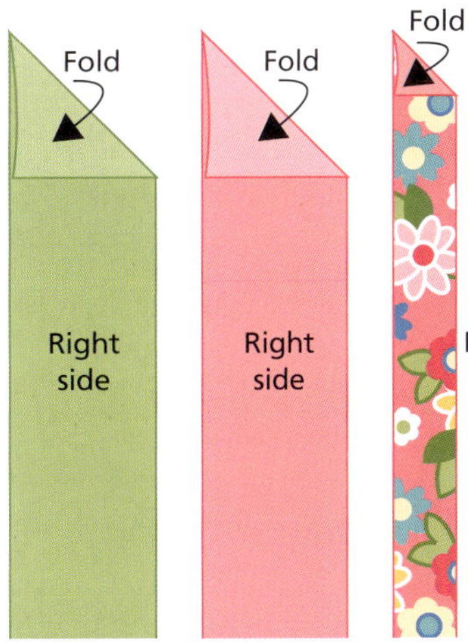

Figure 3

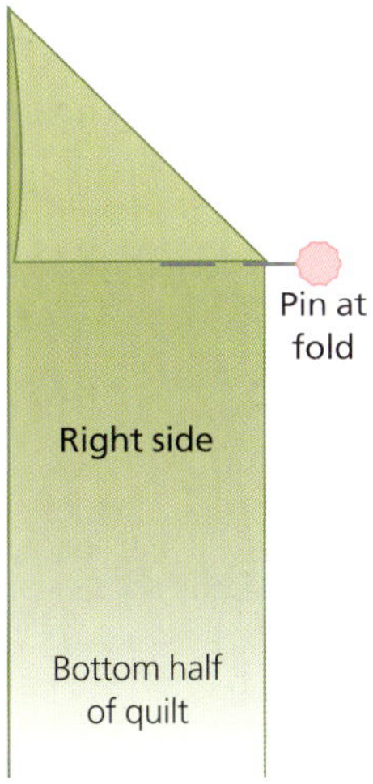

Figure 4

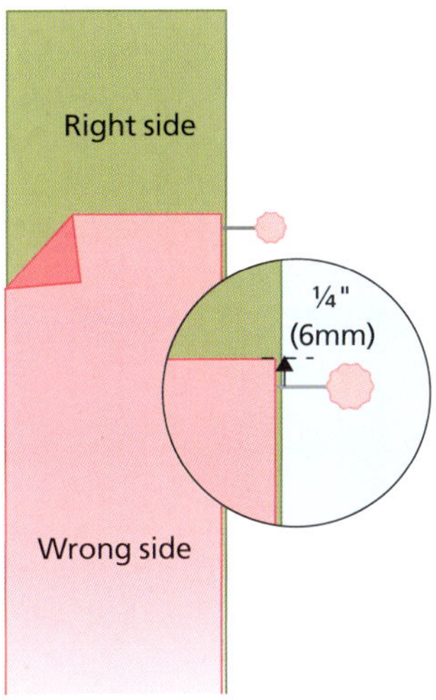

Figure 5

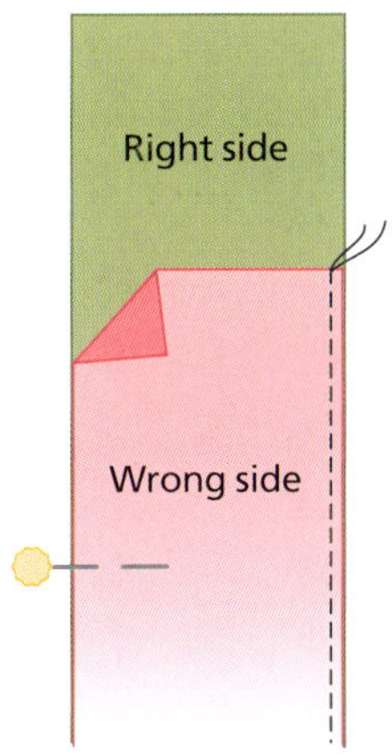

Figure 6

- Add the remaining strips with the same technique, placing each new strip ¼" (6mm) above the pin.
- Stitch strips together from all 3 subsets. Press seam allowances in 1 direction. Figure 7.
- Repeat the process, creating downstairs stratas from 1 grouping of 21"-wide (53.3cm) strips.

4 STITCH UPSTAIRS STRATAS

Upstairs stratas refer to the upward steplike arrangement from left to right.

- Lay out 42" (106.7cm) crosswise strips from 1 grouping, and randomly place the print strips among the solids. (There is no right or wrong arrangement.)
- Rather than sewing all 16 strips (11 solids and 5 prints), create 3 subsets of 5 or 6 pieces.
- Fold the upper *left* corner to the right edge of each strip, creating a 45° angle. Figure 8.
- Place a pin at the fold, then allow the corner to unfold. Repeat for all 16 strips.
- Align 2 strips, right sides together, with the second strip ¼" (6mm) above the pin along the left side. Figure 9.
- Set the sewing machine for a ¼" (6mm) seam allowance *from the left side of the presser foot.*
- Stitch the long edges together.
- Add the remaining strips with the same technique, placing each new strip ¼" (6mm) above the pin.
- Stitch strips together from all 3 subsets. Press seam allowances in 1 direction. Figure 10.
- Repeat the process, creating upstairs stratas from the last grouping of 21" (53.3cm) strips.

Figure 7

Figure 8

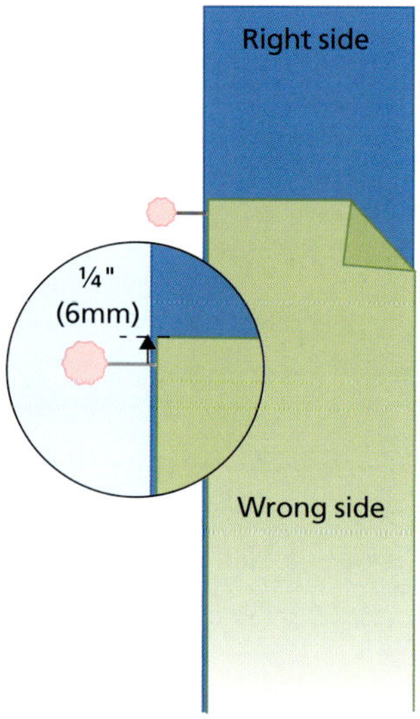

Figure 9

Figure 10

5 CUT CHEVRON SECTIONS

- Mark 45° diagonal lines on the 24" × 36" (61cm × 91.4cm) mat, starting at each upper corner. Use a permanent marker or place masking tape on the mat. Figure 11.
- You will have 6 wide and 3 narrow downstairs stratas. Cut the narrow stratas first.
- Align the left side of 1 narrow downstairs strata along the upper-right-to-lower-left 45° mark. Tape the fabric to the cutting mat.
- Tape two 6" × 24" (15.2cm × 61cm) rulers together, end to end. Place the ruler unit on the mat at the right edge of the strata unit. Align the ruler unit along the *V* shape of the strata and make certain the ruler is straight. Cut off the angled ends, as illustrated. Figure 12.

Note: If you don't have 2 long rulers, borrow 1 from a quilting friend!

- Carefully align the ruler 12" (30.5cm) from the cut edge. Cut along the ruler. Figure 13.

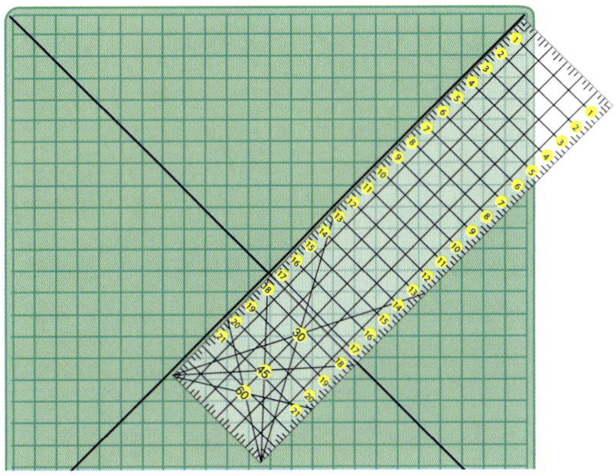

Figure 11

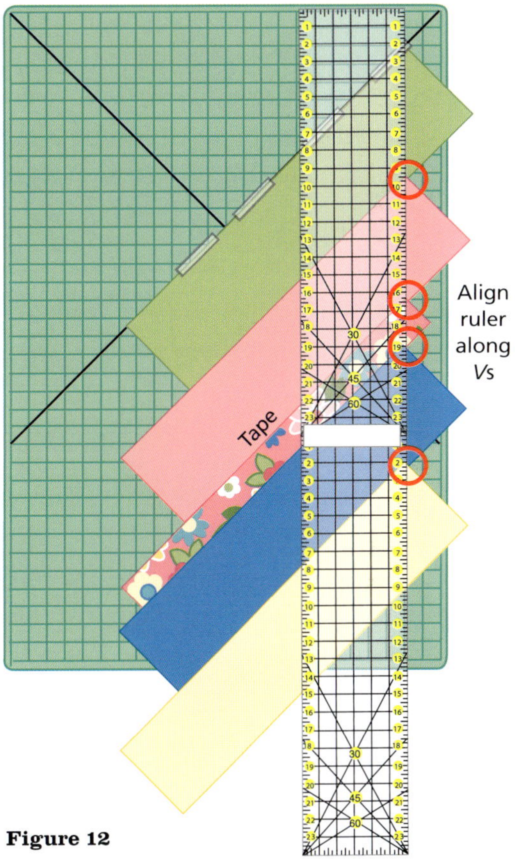

Figure 12

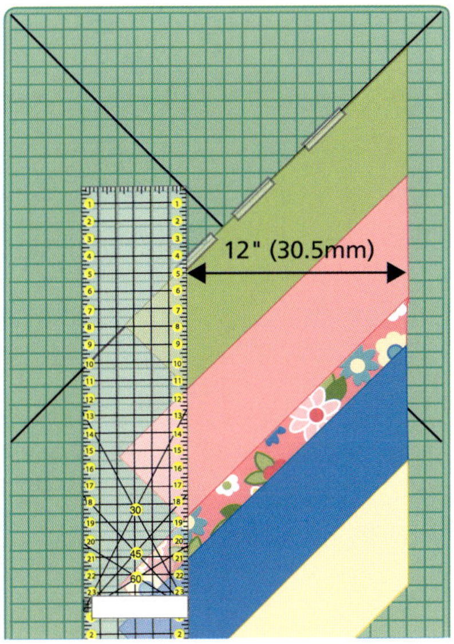

Figure 13

Note: If any of the fabrics you used were narrower than 41" (104.1cm), the 12" (30.5cm) sections may be too wide, meaning that the 12" (30.5cm) measurement may extend beyond the sewn seam. If that is the case, cut the sections narrower to fit within the sewn seams. For example, you might need to cut the sections 11½" (29.2cm) wide. Use that measurement when cutting all the chevron sections.

- Cut all 3 narrow stratas in the same manner.
- You will have 6 wide downstairs stratas remaining. Use the same cutting technique as detailed above, but cut two 12" (30.5cm) sections per strata. Figure 14.
- You will have 6 wide and 3 narrow upstairs stratas. Cut the narrow stratas first.
- Align the right side of 1 narrow upstairs strata along the upper-left-to-lower-right 45° mark. Tape the fabric to cutting mat.
- Place the ruler unit on the mat at the right edge of the strata unit. Align the ruler unit along the *V* shape of the strata and make certain the ruler is straight. Cut off the angled ends, as illustrated. Figure 15.
- Carefully align the ruler 12" (30.5cm) from the cut edge; cut along the ruler.
- Cut all 3 narrow stratas in the same manner.
- You will have 6 wide upstairs stratas remaining. Use the same cutting technique as detailed above, but cut two 12" (30.5cm) columns per strata. Figure 16.

Figure 14

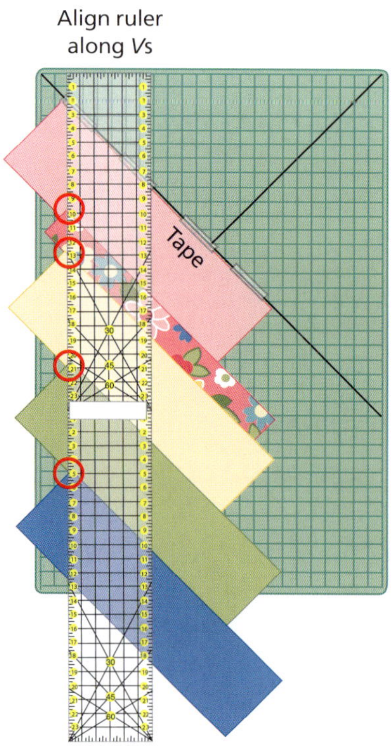

Figure 15

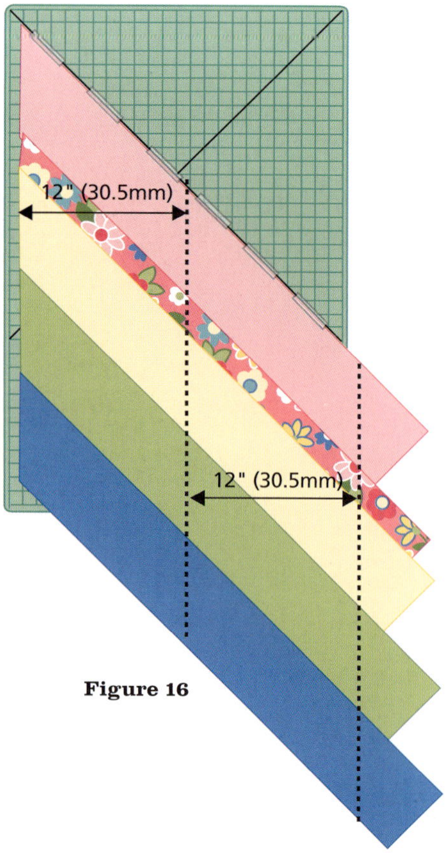

Figure 16

6 CREATE COLUMNS

- Lay out 3 downstairs columns, placing 3 chevron sections per column. Double-check that there are 11 solid and 5 printed chevrons in each column.
- Rearrange the sequence of sections until each column has a unique layout. Figure 17.
- Lay out 3 upstairs columns, placing 3 chevron sections per column. Again, double-check that there are 11 solid and 5 printed chevrons in each column.
- Prearrange the sequence of sections until each column has a unique layout. Figure 18.

7 STITCH COLUMN SECTIONS TOGETHER

- Align the sections of each column with right sides together. Overlap the edges, creating a ¼" (6mm) *V* shape at each end of the seam. Figure 19.
- Stitch a ¼" (6mm) seam allowance, beginning the stitching at the *V* shape created by the overlapped seams. Press.

Note: At this point, the columns have angled ends. Cutting off the excess fabric would be wasteful, plus the columns would become much shorter. The next step creates straight ends, but it involves cutting each column in half and then restitching it. The technique may seem unconventional, but it works!

- Lay 1 column at a time on a cutting mat and align the long edges with the marks on the mat.

Figure 17

Figure 18

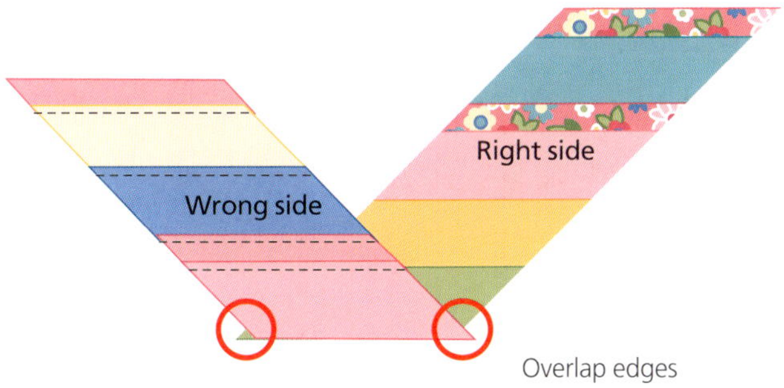

Figure 19

Figure 19

Figure 20

Figure 21

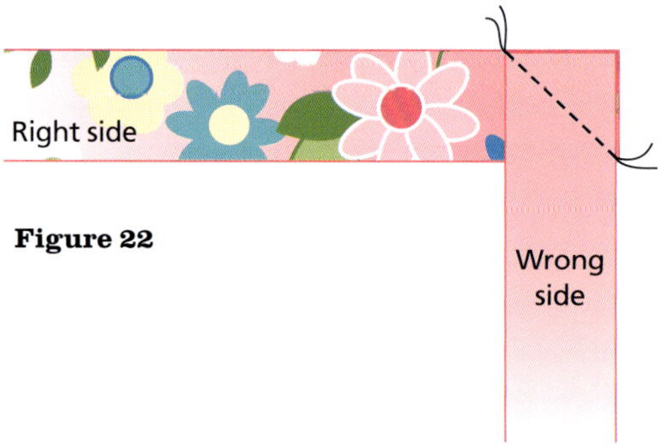

Figure 22

- Place a ruler across the column at any position. Or look for a seam that is less than perfect and place the ruler in that area. Cut across the column. Figure 19.
- Move the lower section above the top section. Stitch the 2 angled sections together, using the same technique detailed above. The column is now a rectangle! Figure 20.
- Repeat for all 6 columns. Figure 21.

8 PIECE NARROW COLUMNS

- Thirty-two 2½" (6.4cm) print strips were set aside for the narrow columns, borders and binding. Count out 22 strips for the narrow columns and borders.
- Join the strips at the short end, right sides together, with a diagonal seam to reduce bulk. Figure 22.
- Trim seams to ¼" (6mm); press seams open.

9 CUT NARROW COLUMNS

- Measure the length of the columns. In this quilt, the columns measure 84" (213.4cm).

Figure 23

Figure 24

- Cut 7 narrow columns the same length as the chevron columns.
- Quarter mark the long edges of the chevron and narrow columns. To do this, fold each length in half, meeting the short ends; fold a second time. Place a pin at each fold.
- Pin a narrow column to the left side of each chevron column, matching quarter marks; stitch. Figure 23.
- Stitch the remaining narrow column to the far right column. Press the seams. Figure 24.

10 STITCH THE COLUMNS

- Pin and stitch the columns, using a ¼" (6mm) seam allowance. Press the seams.
- Measure the top and lower edges. Cut 2 lengths from the print fabric.
- Stitch the borders to the top and lower edges of the quilt top; press.

11 LAYER, QUILT AND BIND

- Use your favorite methods or refer to pages 114–121.
- Use the print binding strips for the binding.

NOTE FROM NANCY

Generally it isn't necessary to pin crosswise strips before stitching. Since the edges of the chevron columns are on the bias and may stretch, this quarter-marking and pinning technique keeps the bias edges from stretching.

21½" × 71" (54.6cm × 180.3cm)

CHAPTER NINE

Hit-and-Miss Table Runner

At first glance, hexagon shapes cause many quilters to think, "Oh no, I dread Y-seams!" Not so with this speedy columns quilt design. The hexagon shapes are created with two halves, thereby eliminating the intersection of three seams, otherwise known as Y-seams. With this technique, faux hexagon halves are stitched in columns with relative speed and ease. The results are dramatic.

FINISHED SIZE

- Approximately 21½" × 71" (54.6cm × 180.3cm)

SUPPLIES

- 1½ yards (1.4m) Fabric A (gray) for column strips
- ⅛ yard (.1m) Fabric B (yellow) for hexagon blocks
- ⅛ yard (.1m) Fabric C (lime) for hexagon blocks
- ⅛ yard (.1m) Fabric D (aqua) for hexagon blocks
- ⅛ yard (.1m) Fabric E (navy) for hexagon blocks
- 2 yards (1.8m) Fabric F (turquoise) for hexagon blocks, backing and binding
- 26" × 75" (66.0cm × 190.5cm) batting
- Fine-point fabric marking pen
- Essential Quilting Tools (see listing on page 110)
- Trace 'n Create Quilt Templates (Faux Hexagon Template—Grandmother's One-Patch Collection) or paper templates on page 122.

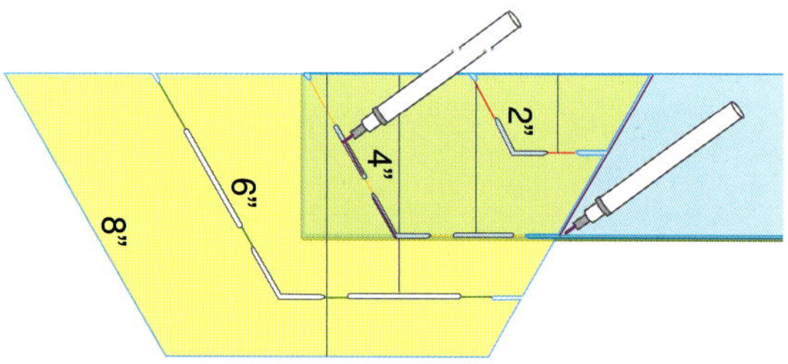

Figure 1

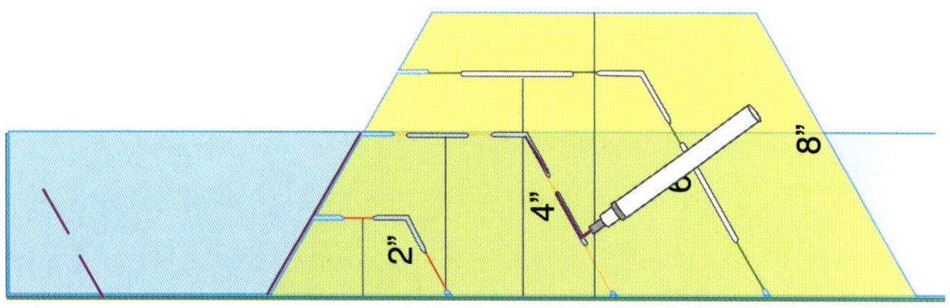

Figure 2

Note: All seam allowances are ¼" (6mm) unless otherwise stated.

1 PREPARE AND CUT FABRICS

- Press and stabilize the fabric with spray starch or a starch alternative, such as Best Press Starch Alternative. See page 112.
- Fabric A (gray): Cut twelve 4" (10.2cm) crosswise strips.
- Fabric B (yellow): Cut one 4" (10.2cm) crosswise strip.
- Fabric C (lime): Cut one 4" (10.2cm) crosswise strip.
- Fabric D (aqua): Cut one 4" (10.2cm) crosswise strip.
- Fabric E (navy): Cut one 4" (10.2cm) crosswise strip.
- Fabric F (turquoise):
  - Cut one 4" (10.2cm) crosswise strip for the half hexagon blocks.
  - Cut five 2½" (6.4cm) crosswise strips for binding.
  - Cut two 26" (66.0cm) crosswise strips for backing.

2 TRACE AND CUT HALF HEXAGON BLOCKS

- Set aside 1 Fabric A (gray) strip.
- Layer two to four 4"-wide (10.2cm) fabric strips for the half hexagon blocks.
- Align the straight edge of the template along the long edges of the stacked fabric strips. Trace the side markings for the 4" (10.2cm) block size. Use a fine-point fabric marking pen. Figure 1.
- Rotate the template, as needed. Align the diagonal line of the template to the line marked on the fabric and along the straight edges of the fabric. Trace the side of the template. Figure 2.
- Repeat stacking and tracing until enough fabric shapes have been traced to complete

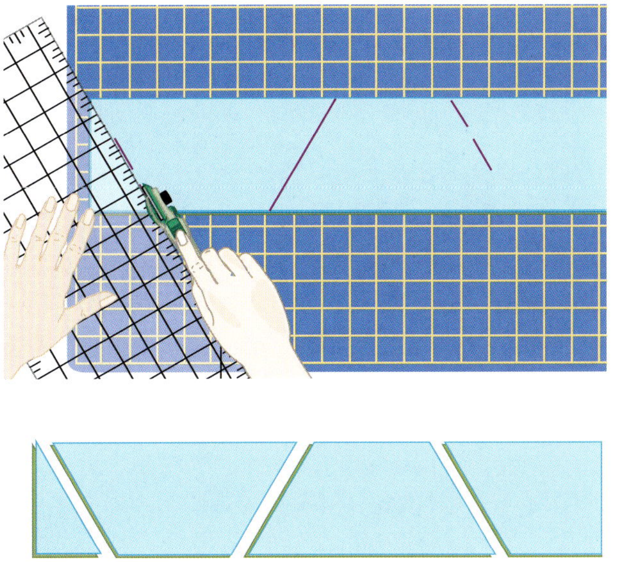

Figure 3

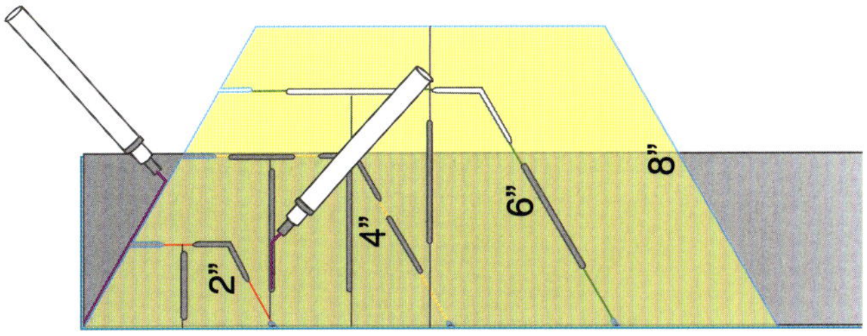

Figure 4

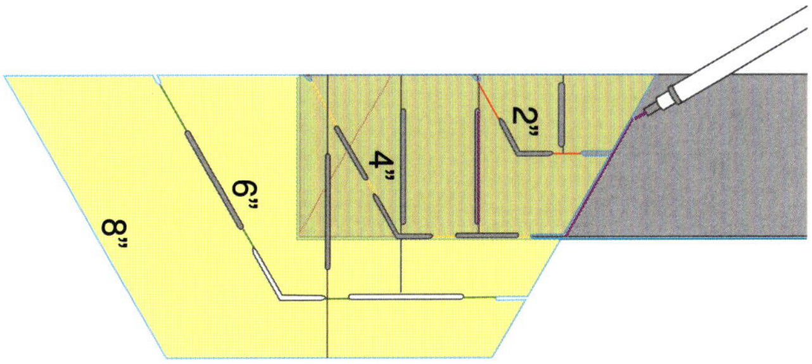

Figure 5

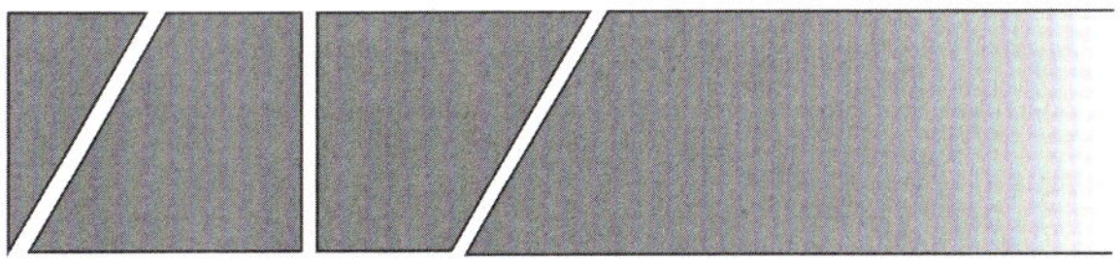

Figure 6

the quilt project, following Figure 7 on page 68.

- Align a ruler along each vertical marking, and use a rotary cutter and mat to cut the shapes. Figure 3.

3 TRACE AND CUT FINISHING PIECES

- Align the straight edge of the template along a long edge of the Fabric A strip that was set aside. With a fine-point fabric marking pen, trace the side marking for the 4" (10.2cm) block size within the die-cut areas of the Finishing Piece. Figure 4. Or use the Finishing Pieces template on page 122. Each column has finishing pieces at top and bottom.
- Rotate the template. Align the die-cut area of the template to the line marked on the fabric. Trace the side of the template. Repeat the process, tracing a total of 12 Finishing Pieces, 6 slanting down to the left and 6 slanting down to the right. Figure 5.
- Align a ruler along each marking and accurately make the cut with a rotary cutter. Figure 6.

NOTE FROM NANCY

The templates on page 122 yield a 4" (10.2cm) hexagon. If you're using the Faux Hexagon shape from the Trace 'n Create Quilt Template—Grandmother's One-Patch Collection, there are 3 more options: 2" (5.1cm), 6" (15.2cm) and 8" (20.3cm). You can customize the size of this table runner by using different shapes.

4 LAY OUT SHAPES FOR THE HEXAGON DESIGNS

- Lay out the pieces in each column to create the design. Figure 7. Or choose a layout design to your liking.
- Place Finishing Pieces at the top and bottom of each column. Figure 8.

5 JOIN PIECES FOR EACH COLUMN

- Place the first 2 pieces, right sides together, and extend the seam allowances ¼" (6mm) to create a *V* shape. Figure 9.
- Align the edge of the presser foot with the edge of the fabric. Stitch the seam. The first and last stitches should land at the *V* shapes of the seam allowance. Figure 10.

NOTE FROM NANCY

A table runner is an ideal project for using scraps of batting. Use a batting tape, such as Pellon's Batting Tape, to gently press batting edges together (see page 115).

Figure 7

Figure 8 Place Finishing Pieces

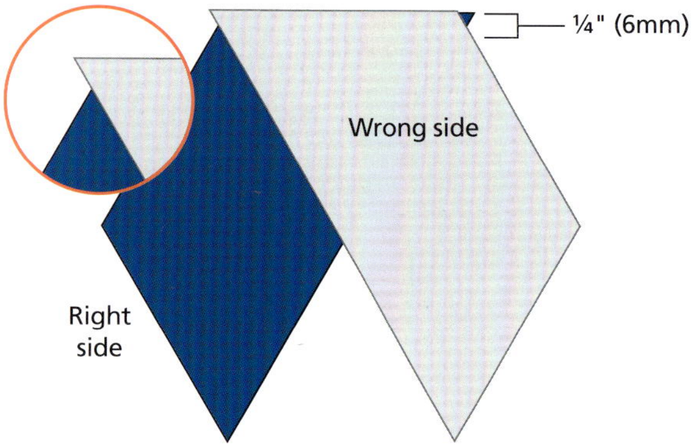

Figure 9

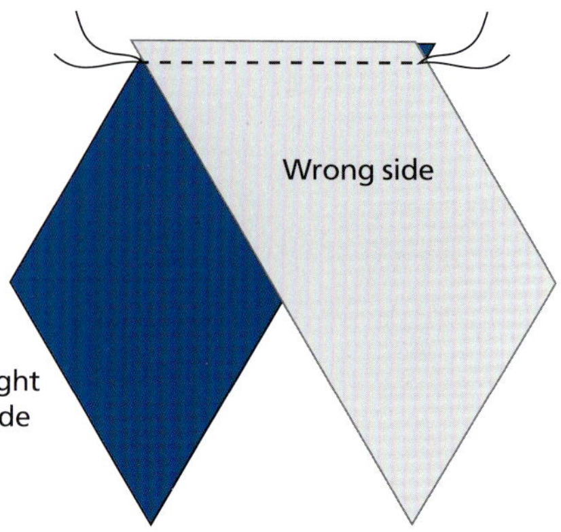

Figure 10

- Press the seam open. Figure 11.
- Place fabrics right sides together and stitch the remaining seams in the first column. Figure 12.
- Repeat until all columns have been pieced.
- Join columns vertically, with right sides together and match seams as you stitch. Press seams open. Figure 13.

6 LAYER, QUILT AND BIND

- Use your favorite methods or refer to pages 114–121.
- Use Fabric F binding strips for the binding.

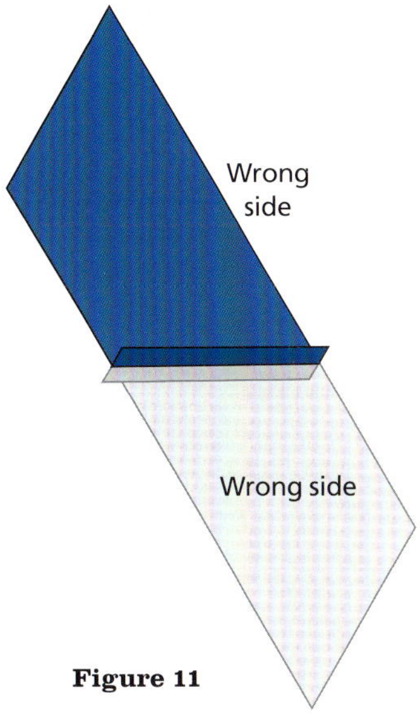

Figure 11

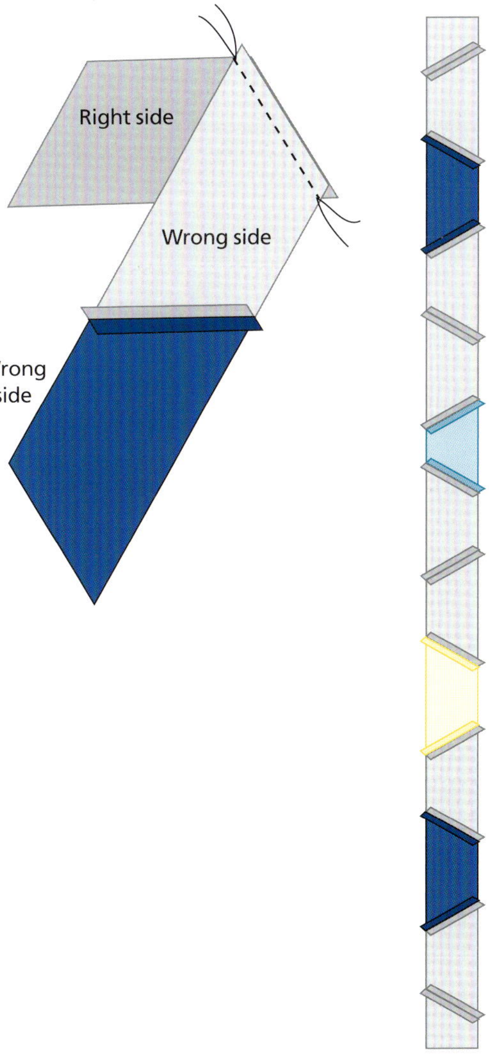

Figure 12

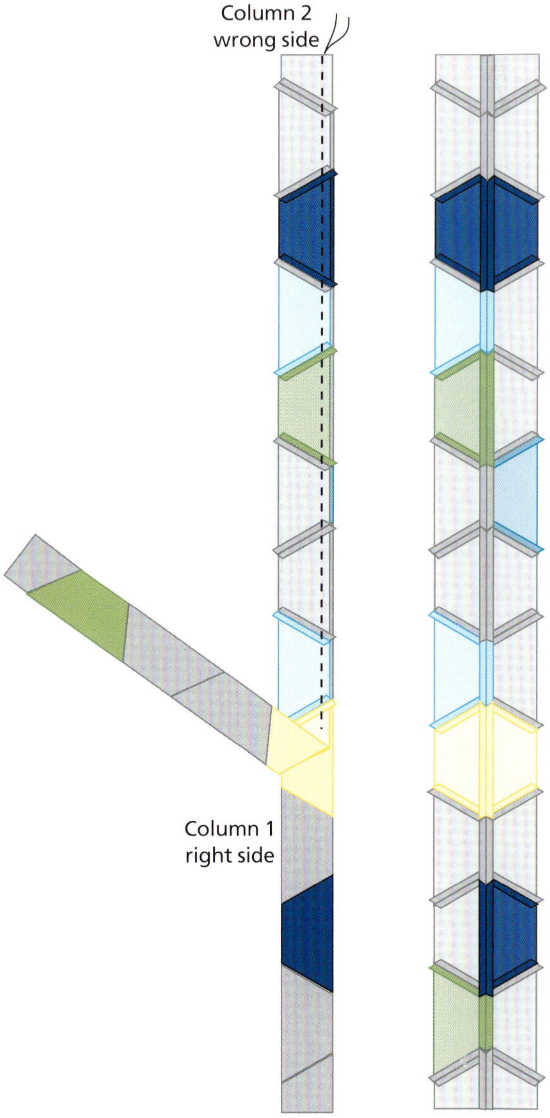

Figure 13

68" × 88" (172.7cm × 223.5cm)

CHAPTER TEN

Tumbling Tumblers Column Quilt

Quilts made from tumbler templates were often scrap quilts with the shapes pieced into rows. Take a speedy approach to this time-honored quilt block. Rotate the shapes 90° to create columns, not rows. Include varied column sizes, and turn what was traditional into a modern *Tumbling Tumblers Column Quilt*.

FINISHED SIZE

- Approximately 68" × 88" (172.7cm × 223.5cm)

SUPPLIES

- 4⅝ yards (4.2m) Fabric A for narrow accent columns, background tumblers and binding
- ⅞ yard (.8m) each of 7 cotton Fabrics B–H for accent tumblers
- Twin-size batting (72" × 90"/ 182.9cm × 228.6cm)
- Fine-point fabric marking pen or a pencil
- Essential Quilting Tools (see listing on page 110)
- Trace 'n Create Quilt Templates (Multisized Tumbler Template—Grandmother's One-Patch Collection) or paper templates in 4 sizes 4" (10.2cm), 6" (15.2cm), 8" (20.3cm) and 10" (25.4cm) on page 123.

Note: All seam allowances are ¼" (6mm) unless otherwise stated.

1 PREPARE FABRICS AND CUT FABRIC A

Stabilize all fabrics well using spray starch or a starch alternative, such as Mary Ellen's Best Press. See page 112.

- Cut Fabric A strips for narrow accent columns. Figure 1.
  - Cut nine 2½" (6.4cm) crosswise strips.
  - Cut seven 3½" (8.9cm) crosswise strips.
  - Cut three 4½" (11.4cm) crosswise strips.
- Cut Fabric A strips for background tumbler pieces. Figure 2.
  - Cut three 4½" (11.4cm) crosswise strips.
  - Cut three 6½" (16.5cm) crosswise strips.
  - Cut three 8½" (21.6cm) crosswise strips.
  - Cut two 10½" (26.7cm) crosswise strips.
- Cut eight 2½" (6.4cm) crosswise strips for binding. Set aside.

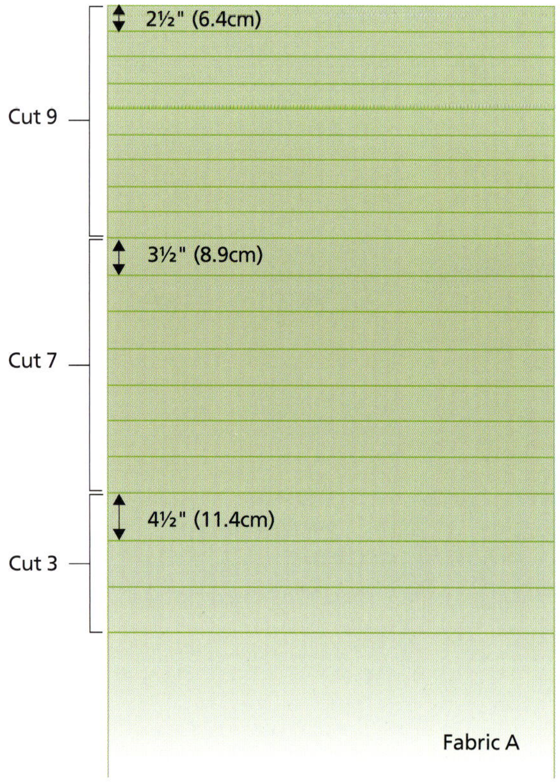

Figure 1

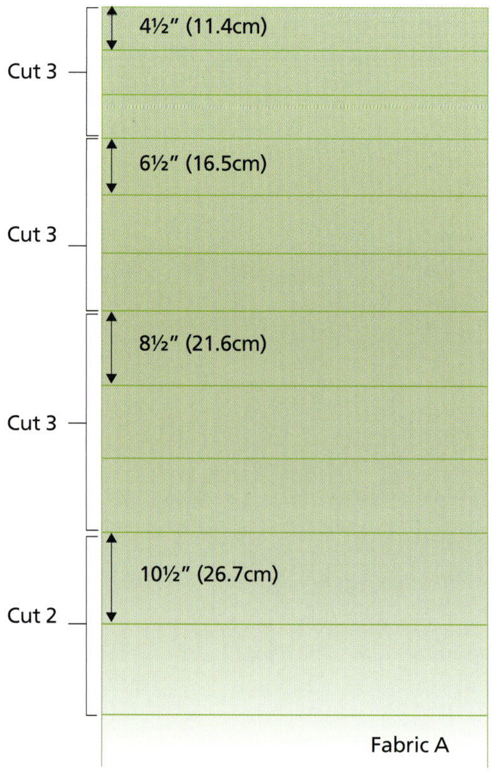

Figure 2

2 CUT FABRICS B–H

- Cut each of the 7 fabric colors into 4 crosswise strips for accent tumblers in the following widths. Figure 3.
  - Cut one 4½" (11.4cm) crosswise strip from each of the colors B–H.
  - Cut one 6½" (16.5cm) crosswise strip from each of the colors B–H.
  - Cut one 8½" (21.6cm) crosswise strip from each of the colors B–H.
  - Cut one 10½" (26.7cm) crosswise strip from each of the colors B–H.

3 STITCH 8 NARROW CROSSWISE COLUMNS FROM FABRIC A

- Create four 2½"-wide (6.4cm) strips for narrow crosswise columns. To do this, fold one 2½" (6.4cm) strip in half, and then in half again. Cut along the folds to create 4 sections. Each section is approximately 10" (25.4cm) in length.
- Create 4 stacks of strips: Each stack will consist of 2 full-length strips and one 10" (25.4cm) strip.
- Stitch 2 full-length strips and one 10" (25.4cm) strip from each of the 4 stacks. Seam the short ends right sides together. Press the seams. Figure 4.
- Create three 3½"-wide (8.9cm) narrow columns. To do this, fold one 3½" (8.9cm) crosswise strip in half, and then in half again. Cut along the folds to create 4 sections, each approximately 10" (25.4cm) in length. Only 3 of the 4 lengths will be used. Set aside the remaining 10" (25.4cm) length for your fabric stash.
- Create 3 stacks of strips. Each stack will consist of 2 full-length strips and one 10" (25.4cm) strip.
- Stitch the strips together, seaming the short ends; press seams. Figure 5.
- Create one 4½"-wide (11.4cm) narrow column. To do this, cut a 10" (25.4cm) length from 1 of the crosswise strips. Set aside the remaining length, approximately 30" (76.2cm) for your fabric stash.
- Stitch the strips (2 full-length strips and the 10" [25.4cm] strip) together, seaming the short ends; press seams. Figure 6.

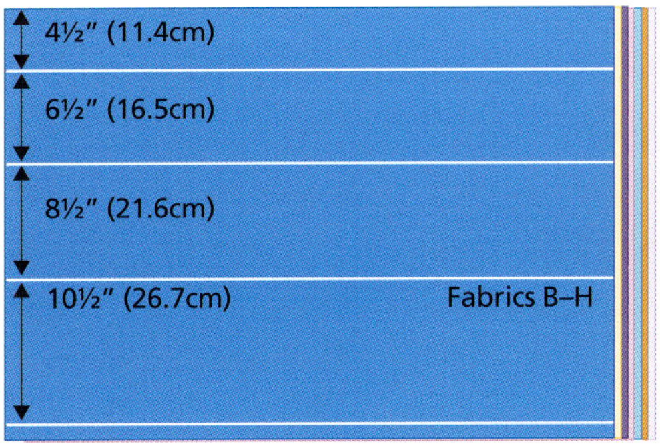

Figure 3

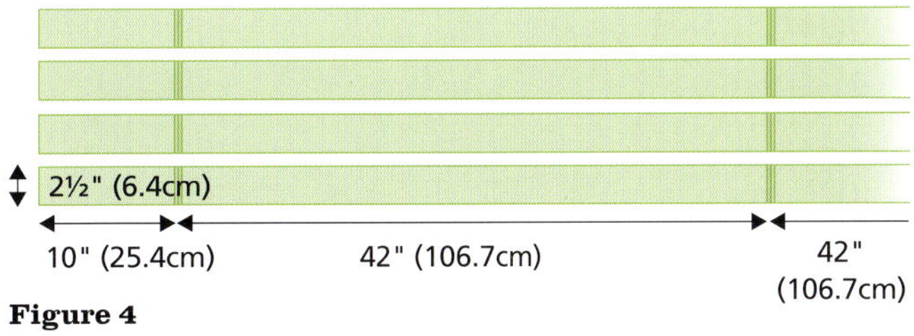

Figure 4

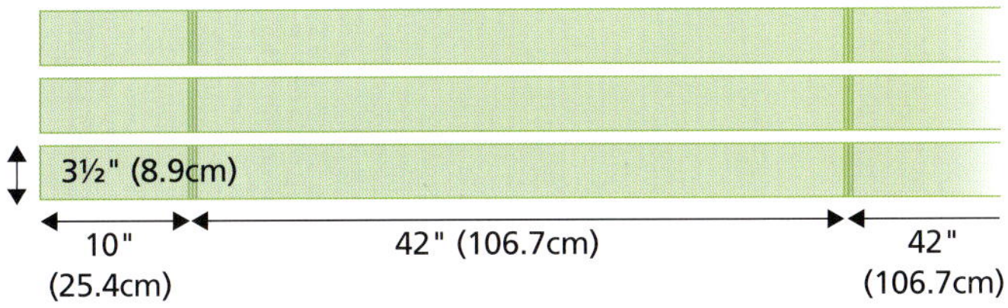

Figure 5

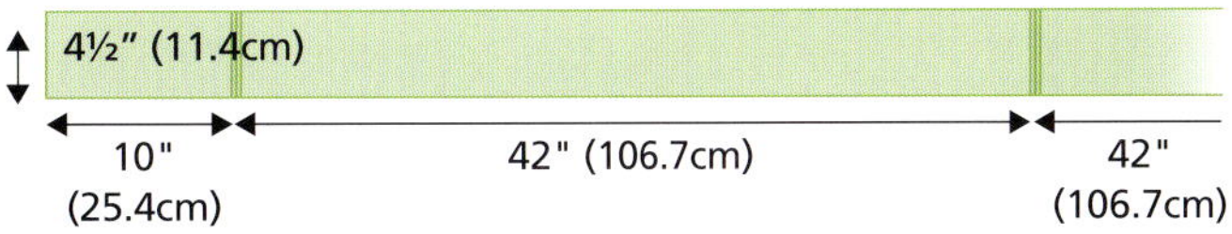

Figure 6

4 TRACE AND THEN CUT TUMBLER SHAPES

- Stack fabric strips B–H.
- Align the straight edge of the template along the long edges of the stacked fabric strips. Trace the side markings for the selected tumbler size using a fine-point fabric marking pen or a pencil. Figure 7.
- Rotate the template. Align the diagonal line of the template to the line marked on the fabric and the straight edge along the straight edge of the fabric. Trace the side of the template. Figure 8.
- Repeat tracing until enough shapes have been traced to complete the quilt project.
- Align a ruler along each vertical marking and accurately make the cut with a rotary cutter. Figure 9.

5 LAY OUT 7 TUMBLER COLUMNS

- The featured twin-size quilt has the following number of tumbler pieces per column:
  - Two 4" (10.2cm) tumbler columns, each with 40 tumbler pieces.
  - Two 6" (15.2cm) tumbler columns, each with 26 tumbler pieces.
  - Two 8" (20.3cm) tumbler columns, each with 20 tumbler pieces.
  - One 10" (25.4cm) tumbler column with 18 tumbler pieces.

NOTE FROM NANCY

You will cut more tumbler shapes than are needed. Depending on your color choices, you may choose to have more or fewer background-colored tumblers. Later in the directions, you'll determine the exact number of tumblers per column so that you can arrange the order and choose the color of tumblers to your liking.

You can use the extra pieces to make a matching pillow or the quilt backing. See instructions on page 114 for a scrappy quilt backing.

NOTE FROM NANCY

The following chart shows the number of tumblers that can be traced onto a crosswise strip of fabric.

- 4½" (11.4cm) crosswise strip = 12 tumblers (4"/ 10.2cm)
- 6½" (16.5cm) crosswise strip = 8 tumblers (6"/ 15.2cm)
- 8½" (21.6cm) crosswise strip = 6 tumblers (8"/ 20.3cm)
- 10½" (26.7cm) crosswise strip = 5 tumblers (10"/ 25.4cm)

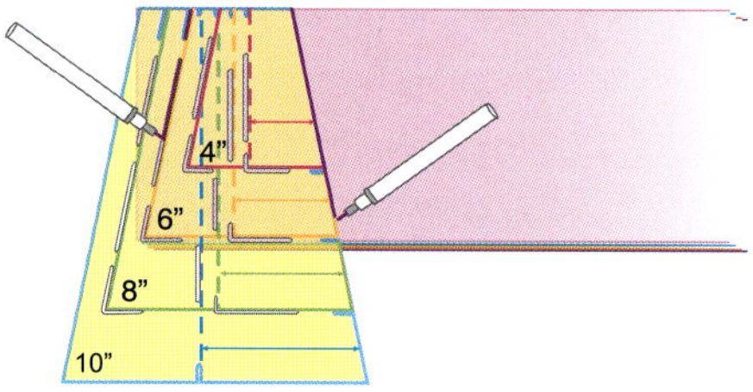

Figure 7

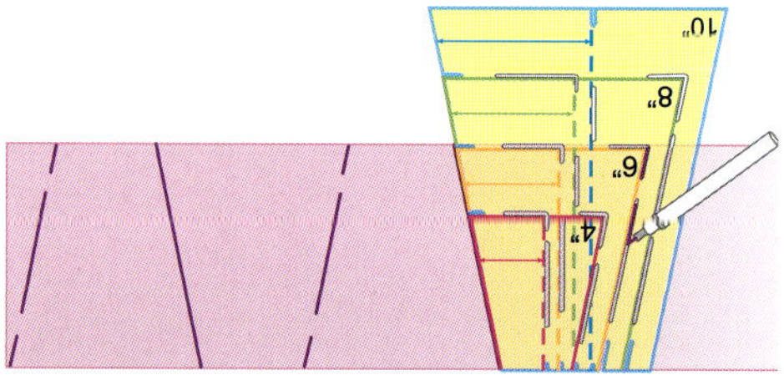

Figure 8

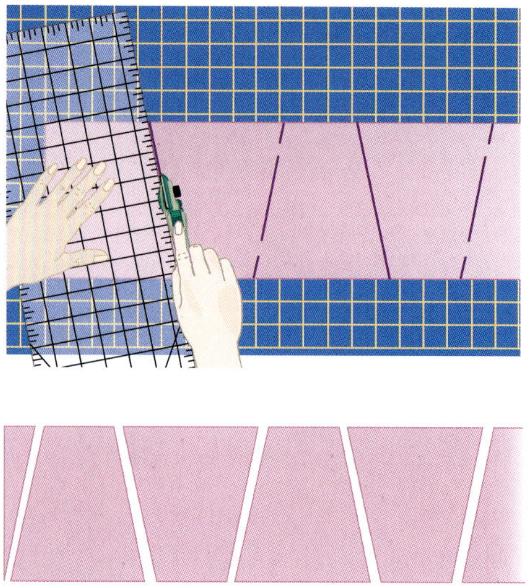

Figure 9

- Choose tumbler pieces for each column. Select a variety of accent fabrics and background fabrics.

6 STITCH TUMBLER COLUMNS AND PRESS SEAMS OPEN

- Stitch pieces of each column together. To do this, align the right sides and edges of the tumbler shapes, extending the seam allowance ¼" (6mm), creating a slight *V* shape.
- Align the edge of the sewing machine's presser foot with the edge of the fabric. Stitch the seam. The first and the last stitches should land at the *V* shapes created by the overlapping seam allowances (see page 68 for the technique). Press seams open. Figure 10.
- Lay out the columns, according to Figure 11. Position the narrow columns between the tumbler columns. Or choose your own order.
- Continue adding columns until the size of the patchwork is complete.

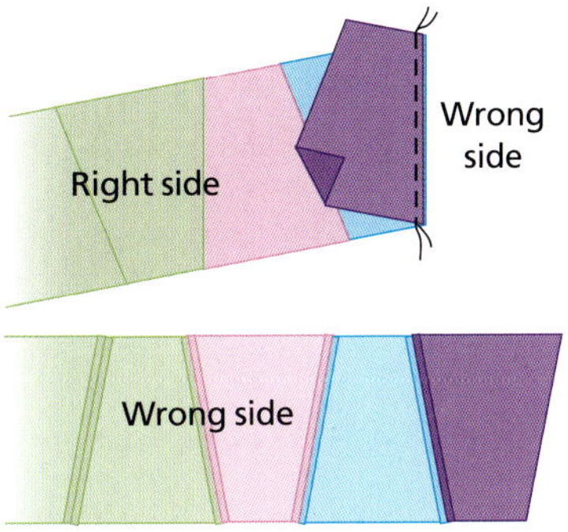

Figure 10

Figure 11

NOTE FROM NANCY

When making this quilt top, I used graph paper to determine the layout of the tumbler blocks. You could also lay the pieces on the floor or on a ping-pong table. This is a very visual process with no wrong answer!

- Trim all lengths to 90" (228.6cm). Figure 12.
- Stitch the narrow columns to the tumbler columns.
- Stitch all columns together. Figure 13.

7 CREATE A SCRAPPY QUILT BACKING, IF DESIRED

- Use some of the pieces that weren't needed for the quilt to make the backing. Figure 14.

8 LAYER, QUILT AND BIND

- Use your favorite methods or refer to pages 114–121.
- Use Fabric A binding strips for the binding.

NOTE FROM NANCY

Since trimming the columns isn't an exact science, I found it important to shift some columns up and some down to get a visually pleasing layout. That's why I recommend trimming from both the top and the lower edges.

Figure 12

Figure 13

Figure 14

CREATIVE OPTIONS

Use a monochromatic color scheme to make a more subtle statement.

80" × 88" (203.2cm × 223.5cm)

CHAPTER ELEVEN

Floating Squares Column Quilt

This full-size quilt looks like it would be difficult to make, but it is so simple! The darker squares seem to float on the light background of the quilt top. The two-color quilt top consists of ten floating squares columns and eleven narrow columns. First you'll create stratas and then you'll cut and join them to create floating squares columns—easy methods that yield spectacular results!

FINISHED SIZE

- Approximately 80" × 88" (203.2cm × 223.5cm) full/double-size quilt

SUPPLIES

- 1¾ yards (1.6m) Fabric A (blue) for floating squares
- 5⅜ yards (5m) Fabric B (white) for background and narrow columns
- Full/double-size batting
- Essential Quilting Tools (see listing on page 110)

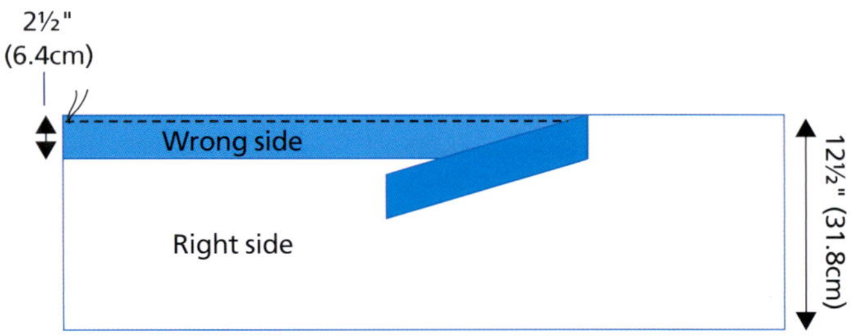

Figure 1

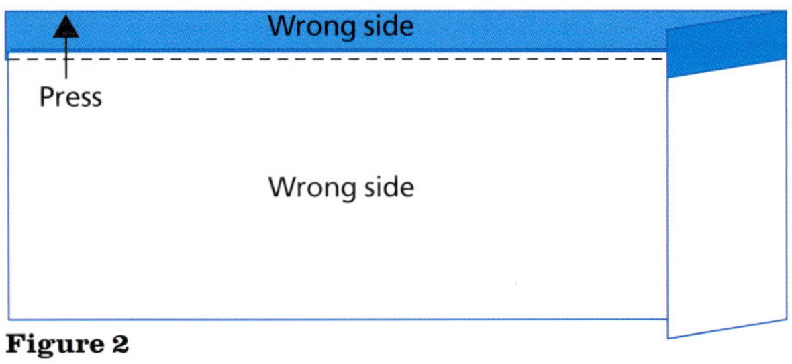

Figure 2

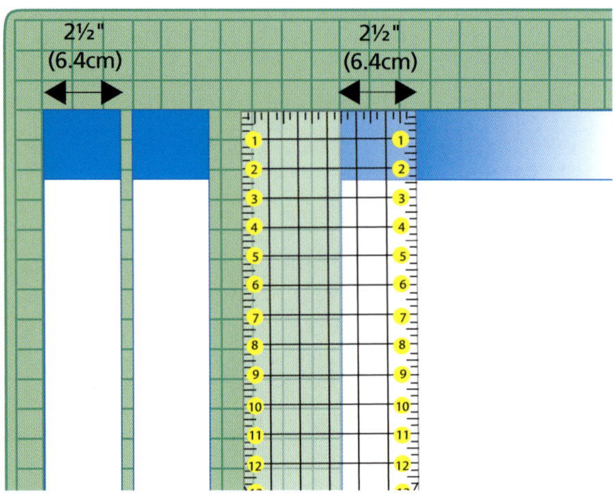

Figure 3

Note: All seam allowances are ¼" (6mm) unless otherwise stated.

1 PREPARE AND CUT FABRIC

- Stabilize all fabrics well using spray starch or a starch alternative, such as Mary Ellen's Best Press. See page 112.
- Fabric A (blue):
  - Cut two 2½" (6.4cm) crosswise strips for floating squares.
  - Cut four 4½" (11.4cm) crosswise strips for floating squares.
  - Cut two 6½" (16.5cm) crosswise strips for floating squares.
  - Cut nine 2½" (6.4cm) crosswise strips for binding.
- Fabric B (white):
  - Cut two 12½" (31.8cm) crosswise strips.
  - Cut four 8½" (21.6cm) crosswise strips.
  - Cut two 10½" (26.7cm) crosswise strips.
  - Cut twenty-four 4½" (11.4cm) crosswise strips for narrow columns; set aside.

2 CREATE SMALL FLOATING SQUARES COLUMNS

- Create 2 stratas of blue/white crosswise strips. Each strata consists of one 2½" (6.4cm) blue strip and one 12½" (31.8cm) white strip.
- Meet right sides and long edges of each pair. Stitch 1 long edge. Figure 1.
- Press the seam toward the blue strip. Figure 2.
- Subcut each strata into 2½"-wide (6.4cm) crosswise strips. Each subset will be 2½" × 14½" (6.4cm × 36.8cm), yielding 32 subsets. Figure 3.
- Place 7 subsets end to end to create 1 column. Stitch the short edges. Figure 4.
- Create a total of four 2½" (6.4cm) floating squares columns. (There will be 4 subsets left over.)
- Press the seams toward the blue fabric.

3 CREATE MEDIUM FLOATING SQUARES COLUMNS

- Create 4 stratas of blue/white crosswise strips. Each strata consists of one 4½" (11.4cm) blue strip and one 8½" (21.6cm) white strip.
- Meet right sides and long edges of each strata. Stitch 1 long edge. Figure 5.
- Press the seams toward the blue fabric.
- Subcut each strata into 4½"-wide (11.4cm) crosswise strips. Each subset will be 4½" × 12½" (11.4cm × 31.8cm), yielding 37 subsets. Figure 6.
- Place 8 subsets end to end to create 1 column. Stitch the short edges. Figure 7.
- Create a total of four 4½" (11.4cm) floating squares columns. (Seven subsets will be left over.) Press the seams toward the blue fabric.

4 CREATE LARGE FLOATING SQUARES COLUMNS

- Create 2 stratas of blue/white crosswise strips. Each strata consists of one 6½" (16.5cm) blue strip and one 10½" (26.7cm) white strip.
- Meet right sides and long edges of each strata. Stitch 1 long edge. Figure 8.

NOTE FROM NANCY

To save time, cut the stratas in pairs. Rotate one strata 180° and stack right sides together to the other strata, as shown, aligning the straight edges as perfectly as possible. (The blue fabric is at the top of one strata and at the bottom of the other strata.) After cutting the subsets, chain stitch the pairs. (Stitch short edges of one pair, then meet a second pair to the first and continue stitching. Repeat until all pairs are joined.) Clip the threads to separate the pairs.

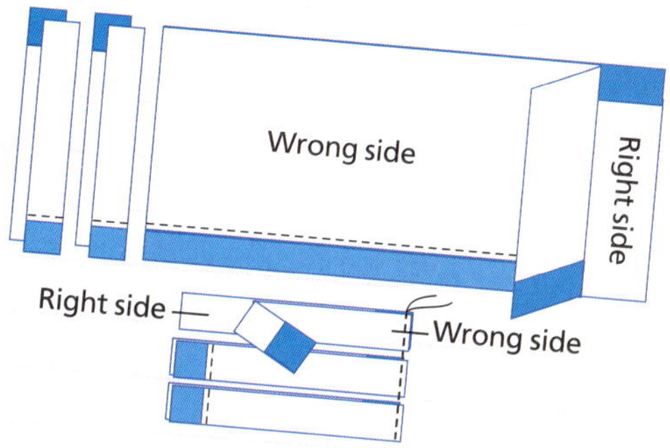

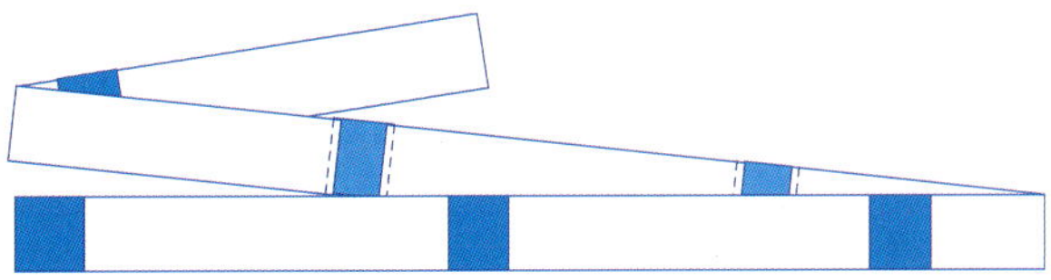

Figure 4

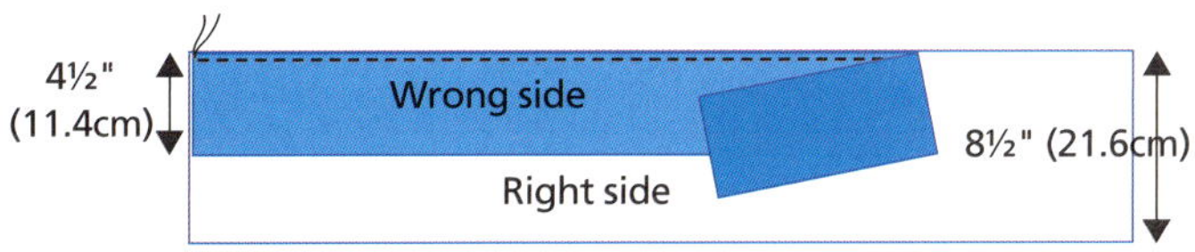

Figure 5

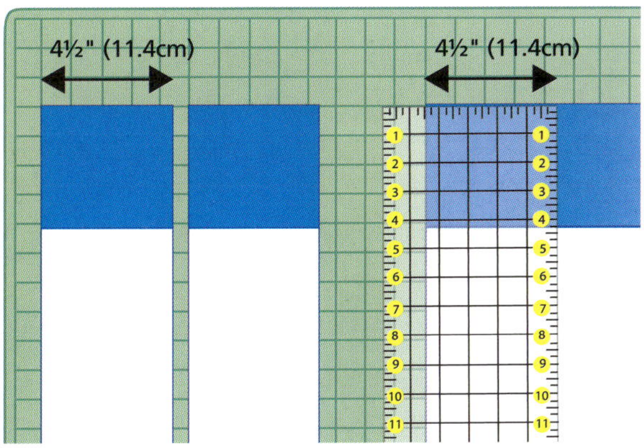

Figure 6

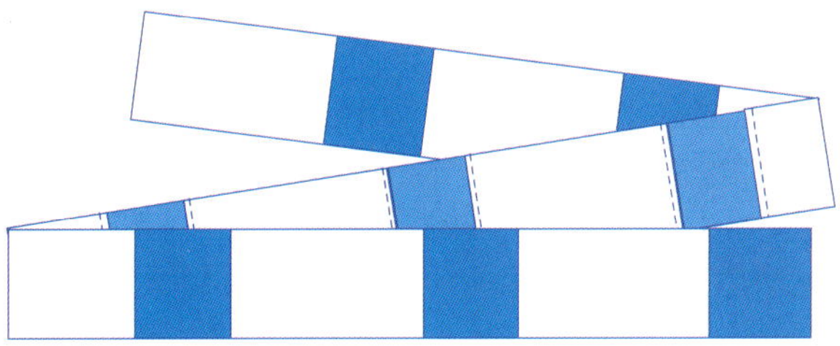

Figure 7

- Press the seams toward the blue fabric.
- Subcut each strata into 6½"-wide (16.5cm) crosswise strips. Each subset will be 6½" × 16½" (16.5cm × 41.9cm), yielding 12 subsets. Figure 9.
- Place 6 subsets end to end to create 1 column. Stitch the short edges.
- Create a total of two 6½" (16.5cm) floating squares columns. (No subsets will be left over.)
- Press the seams toward the blue fabric.

5 STITCH NARROW COLUMNS

- Stitch 4½" (11.4cm) narrow columns end to end; press seam allowances open.
- Cut the long strip into 88" (223.5cm) lengths to create a total of 11 narrow columns. See sidebar on this page.

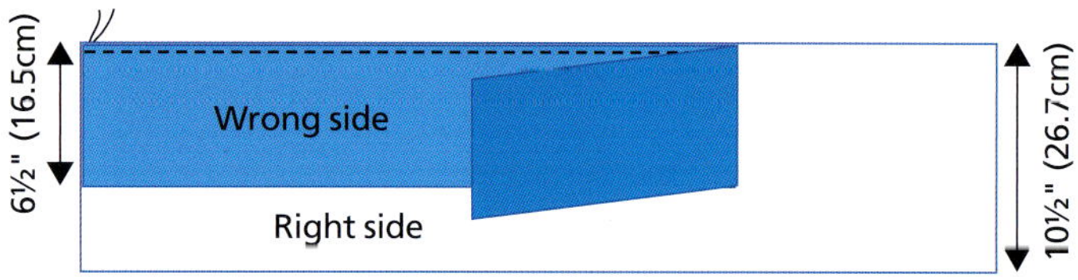

Figure 8

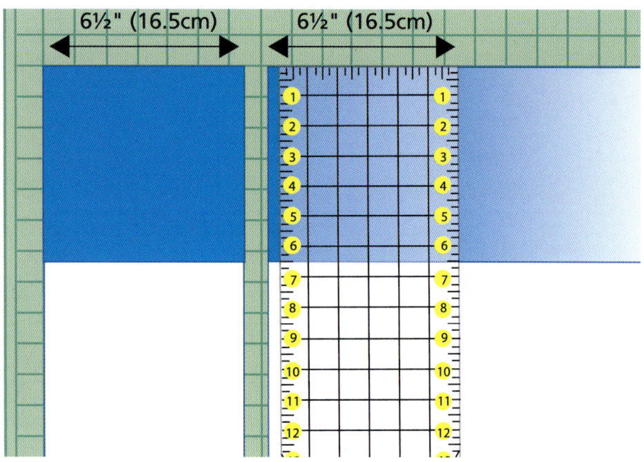

Figure 9

NOTE FROM NANCY

It might be slightly cumbersome to handle twenty-four strips that have been sewn together end to end. Consider stitching three strips together at a time, then cutting an 88" (223.5cm) length strip. Add two or three more strips to the remaining portion of the strip; again cut an 88" (223.5cm) length. Repeat the process until eleven narrow columns have been cut. (The purpose of joining the strips end to end is to avoid fabric waste.)

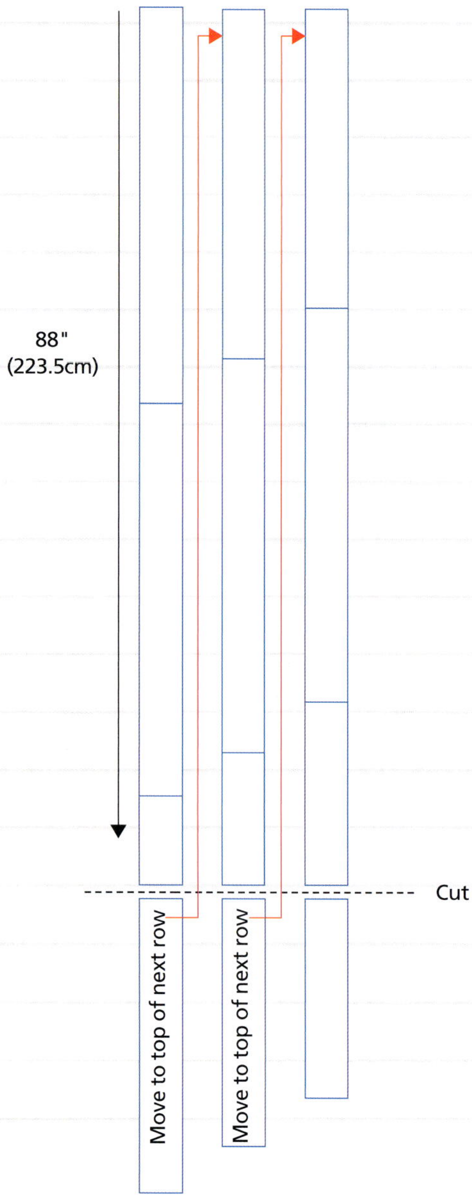

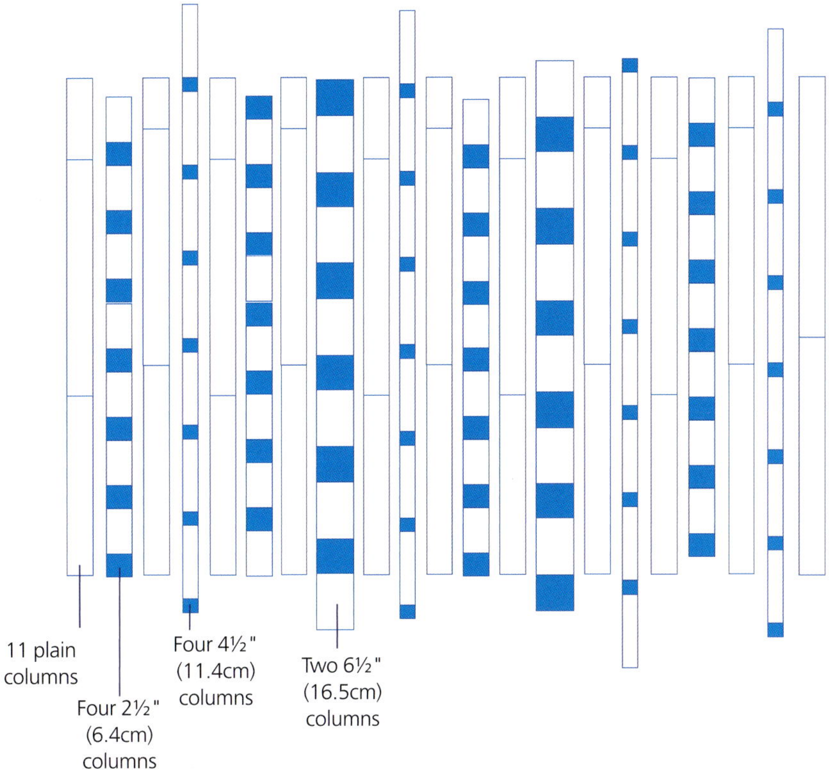

Figure 10

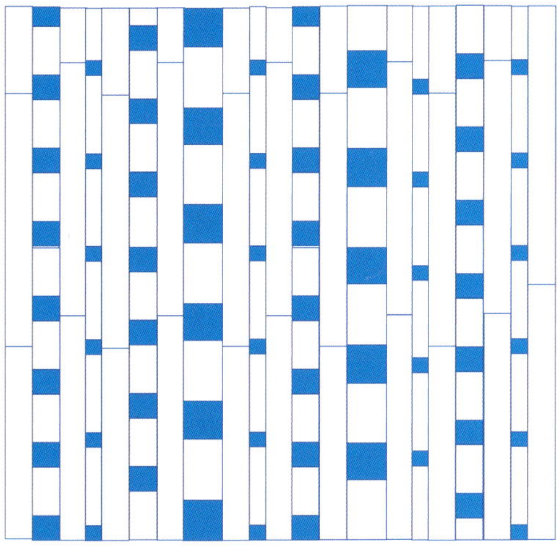

Figure 11

6 LAY OUT COLUMNS

Each of the 3 floating squares column sizes is a different length, and they are all slightly longer than the 88" (223.5cm) finished length of the quilt. This variance in length gives you the option to shift the columns up or down to create a greater effect of floating squares.

- Lay out the columns on a floor or large table so you can mix up the arrangement of the 2½" (6.4cm), 4½" (11.4cm) and 6½" (16.5cm) columns.
- Place a narrow column between each floating column.
- Rotate or shift the square columns up or down so that the blue squares are not lined up across the quilt. Doing so makes the squares appear random or floating. Figure 10.
- Trim all column lengths to 88" (223.5cm).

7 STITCH COLUMNS TO COMPLETE THE QUILT

- Stitch all columns. Press seams open. Figure 11.

8 CREATE A QUILT BACKING

- Use some of the pieces that weren't needed in the quilt to make the backing, if desired.

9 LAYER, QUILT AND BIND

- Use your favorite method or refer to pages 114–121.
- Use Fabric A binding strips for the binding.

NOTE FROM NANCY

Change up the number of columns and the length of the columns for a different size quilt. See a chart of standard sizes for quilts on page 113.

44" × 58" (111.8cm × 147.3cm)

CHAPTER TWELVE

The Original Column Quilt

A worn-out beach towel left behind by a friend provided the inspiration for this quilt. The towel is a jacquard weave, which means it is reversible. The first quilt in this chapter follows the lead of the towel—same coloration and also reversible (without being tattered and worn). The second quilt in this chapter is not reversible and can be made to fit a double, queen or king bed. Both quilt designs are, of course, made of columns, but this time you'll make column units with two solid strips on either side of a patchwork middle strip.

FINISHED SIZE

- Approximately 44" × 58" (111.8cm × 147.3cm), lap or baby's tummy-time quilt

SUPPLIES

- ¾ yard (.7m) Fabric A (purple) for outer strips and center squares
- ¾ yard (.7m) Fabric B (red) for outer strips and center squares
- ¾ yard (.7m) Fabric C (peach) for outer strips and center squares
- 2¼ yards (2.1m) Fabric D (yellow) for outer strips, center squares and borders
- 1¼ yards (1.1m) Fabric E (green) for outer strips, center squares and binding
- ¾ yard (.7m) Fabric F (blue) for outer strips and center squares
- 1 crib- or throw-size package of batting, 60" x 60" (152.4cm x 152.4cm)
- Essential Quilting Tools (see listing on page 110)

NOTE FROM NANCY

Despite its less-than-prime condition, the towel had an interesting design that featured columns of color with square inserts. Once I determined how to piece the center of each column, it was a breeze to create the quilt. I first featured this quilt on *Sewing With Nancy*. The series was so popular that the design became the catalyst for this book!

NOTE FROM NANCY

It isn't necessary to make the quilt reversible. Consider piecing only the top of the quilt, then reduce the fabric yardage by half! Use a single fabric for the backing.

Note: All seam allowances are ¼" (6mm) unless otherwise stated.

1 SELECT FABRICS

- Choose colors of the rainbow, as pictured, or choose complementary colors ranging from light to dark.
- Organize the fabrics in color gradation. Figure 1.
- Reverse the colorations on the back of the quilt. What was the primary column color on the front becomes the secondary color on the back. Figure 2.

2 PREPARE AND CUT FABRICS FOR FRONT AND BACK OF QUILT

- Stabilize all fabrics well using spray starch or a starch alternative such as Mary Ellen's Best Press. See page 112.

From each fabric (Fabrics A–F) cut the following:

- Six 2½" (6.4cm) crosswise strips.
- Two 5" (12.7cm) crosswise strips. Figure 3.
- Reserve the remaining Fabric D for borders. Reserve the remaining Fabric E for the binding.

Figure 1

Figure 2

- Group strips of each color and arrange them in the order in which they will appear in the quilt.

3 PREPARE OUTER STRIPS

- Begin with the primary color fabric in the left column of the quilt front (Fabric A). Cut one 2½" (6.4cm) crosswise strip in half. Figure 4.
- Subcut 1 of the half strips in half again, making 2 strips, each approximately 10½" (26.7cm) long. Figure 5.
- Stitch the short ends of a 2½" × 10½" (6.4cm × 26.7cm) piece to a 2½" × 42" (6.4cm × 106.7cm) crosswise strip of the same color. Create 2 strips. The seamed length is approximately 52"–53" (132.1cm–134.6cm). Press seams flat, then press them open. Figure 6.
- Move the remaining 2½" × 21" (6.4cm × 53.3cm) strip to the fabric grouping of the previous coloration.
- Repeat with each grouping of fabrics. The primary color in the first column becomes the secondary color in the next column. Figure 7.

4 PREPARE THE MIDDLE STRIP OF EACH COLUMN

- Cut the 5" × 42" (12.7cm × 106.7cm) crosswise strip in half, making 2 strips, each approximately 5" × 21" (12.7cm × 53.3cm).

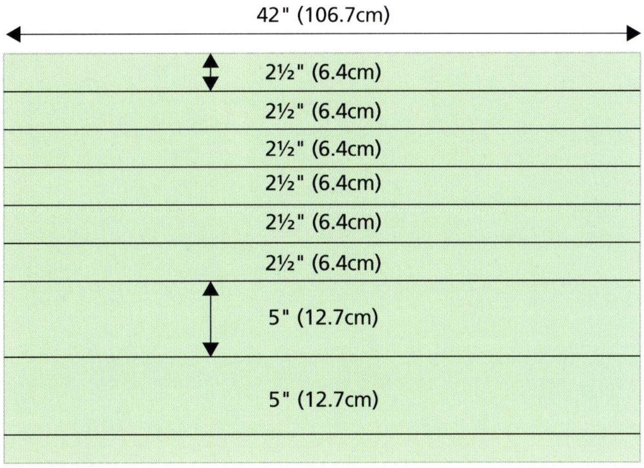

Figure 3

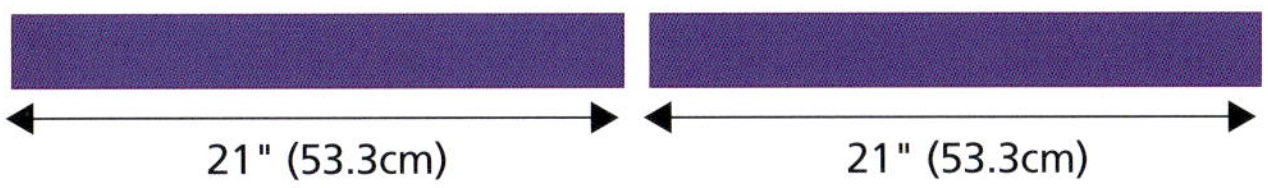

Figure 4

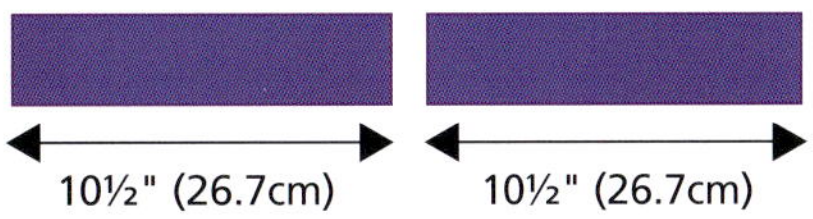

Figure 5

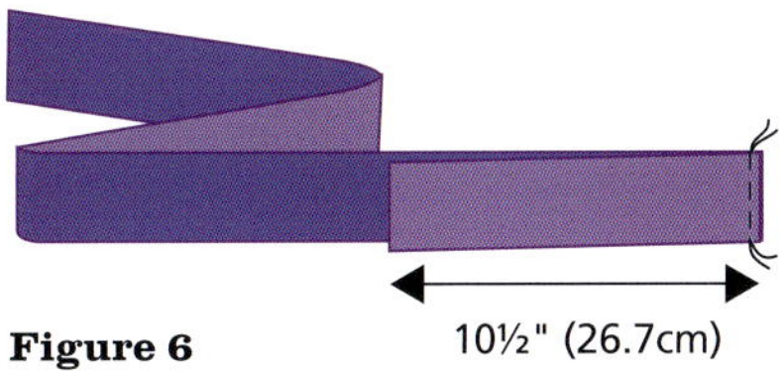

Figure 6

Figure 7

- Prepare a strata by joining lengthwise edges of the primary-colored 5" × 21" (12.7cm × 53.3cm) strip and the secondary-colored 2½" × 21" (6.4m × 53.3cm) strip, right sides together. Figure 8.
- Press the seam flat, then press it to 1 side. Press from the right side to prevent a pleat or tuck from forming next to the seam on the right side of the fabric.
- Subcut the strata into seven 2½" (6.4cm) sections. Figure 9.
- Stitch the short ends of the 2½" (6.4cm) sections with right sides together and alternating colorations. Figure 10.
- Cut a 2½" × 5" (6.4cm × 12.7cm) section from the remaining 5" × 21" (12.7cm × 53.3cm) strip. Join the section to the end of the middle strip so both ends are identical.
- Press the seam flat, then press it away from the center. Press from the right side to prevent a pleat or tuck from forming next to the seam on the right side of the fabric.

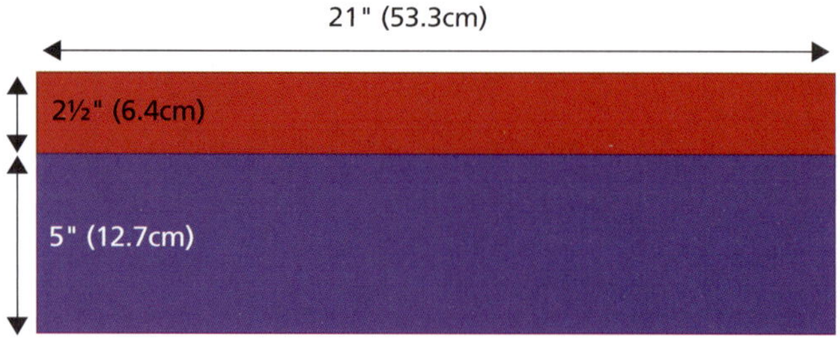

Figure 8

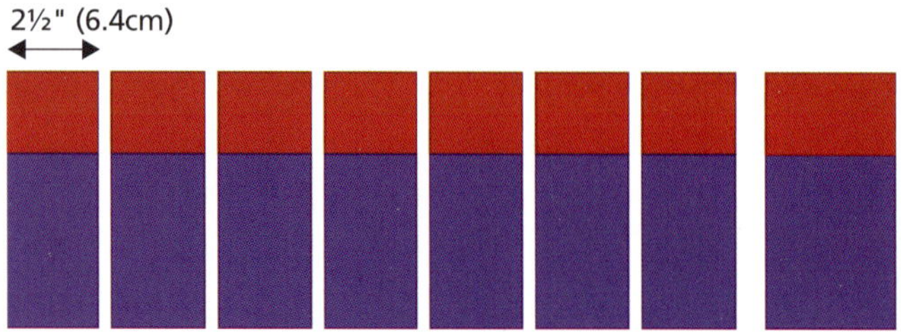

Figure 9

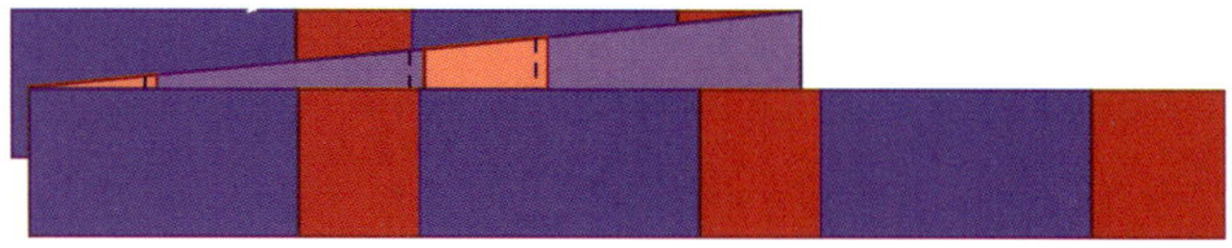

Figure 10

5 STITCH THE MIDDLE STRIP TO THE 2 OUTER STRIPS

- Stitch the middle strip to the 2 outer strips with right sides together. Press the seams flat, then press them away from the center. One column unit is complete. Figure 11.

6 CONTINUE MAKING COLUMN UNITS

- Using the same process, prepare 6 column units for the quilt front and 6 column units for the quilt back.
- Lay out the columns for the front and back of the quilt so what is the primary color of a column on the front is the secondary color of the corresponding column on the back.

7 QUILT AS YOU GO FOR A REVERSIBLE QUILT

- Cut four 6½" (16.5cm) crosswise strips from the batting.
- Trim the length of the batting strips to meet the length of the column units.
- Pin the batting to the wrong side of all 6 front columns. Figure 12.

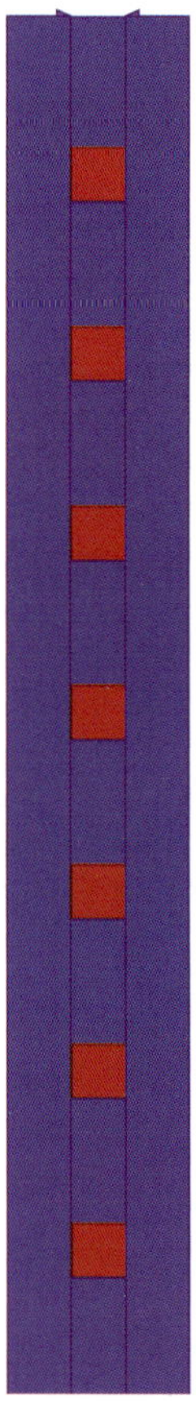

Figure 11

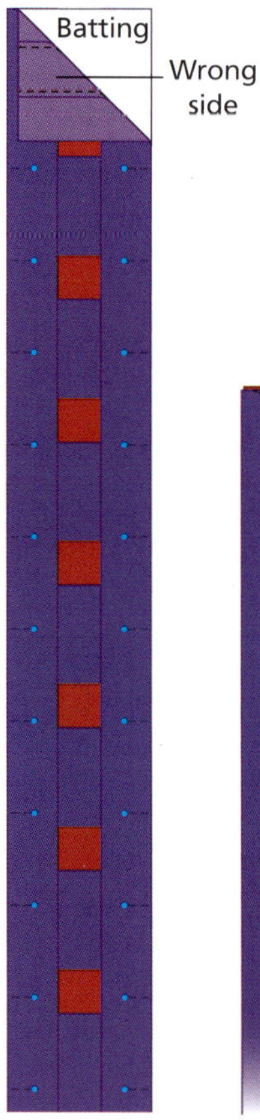

Figure 12

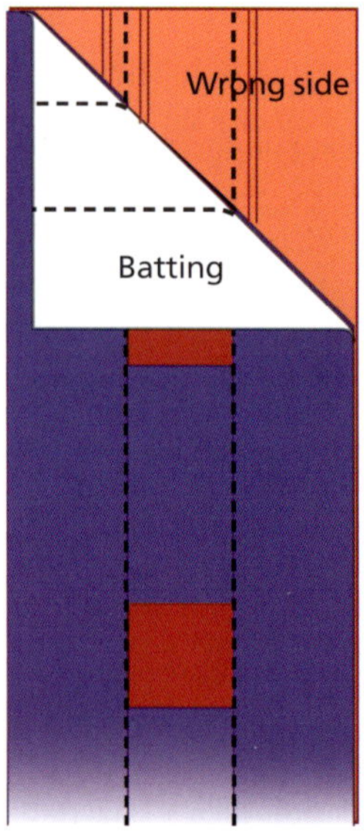

Figure 13

- Stitch in the ditch; that is, sew in the well of the vertical seams on all 6 front column units.
- Align the first front and back columns, wrong sides together. Be sure to match short ends and lengthwise edges. The batting will be sandwiched in the middle of the columns. Figure 13.
- Machine baste a scant ¼" (6mm) from the outer edges. Figure 14.
- Pin the front of Column 2 to the front of Column 1, right sides together. Match long, top and lower edges. Fold back Column 2 to ensure the squares align.
- Pin the back of Column 2 to the back of Column 1, right sides together. Match long edges and make certain the top edges are aligned. Fold back Column 2 to ensure the squares align.
- Stitch a ¼" (6mm) seam joining the front and back of Column 2 to the front and back of Column 1. Because there are multiple layers, slightly lengthen the stitch length. Press seams. Figure 15.
- Unfold the columns. Press the seams and machine baste the lengthwise cut edges together.
- Repeat, adding the front and back of Column 3 to Column 2. Repeat the process to add all remaining column units. Figure 16.

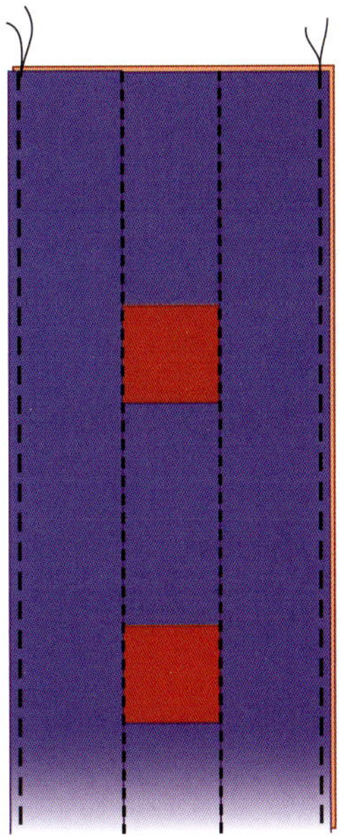
Figure 14

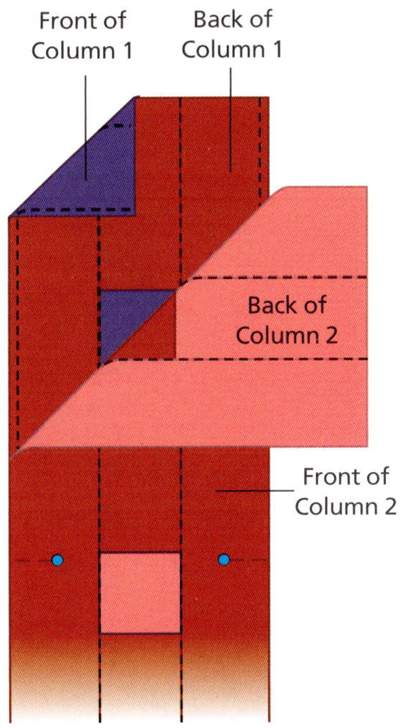

Figure 15

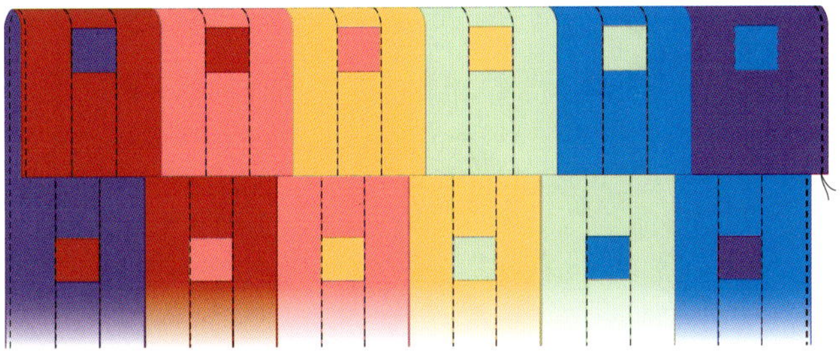
Figure 16

8 ADD THE BORDERS

- Cut ten 4½" × 42" (11.4cm × 106.7cm) Fabric D strips.
- Stitch the short ends of 10 strips, right sides together. Press the seams flat, then press them open.
- Measure the sides of the quilt top.
- Cut 4 borders the length of the side measurement.
- Cut four 4½" (11.4cm) crosswise strips of batting.
- Meet the short ends of the batting and zigzag them together with a wide/long stitch. Or seam the sections together with a lightweight fusible tricot tape, such as Pellon's Batting Tape (see page 115).
- Pin and baste the batting to 2 of the side borders. Trim excess batting.
- Stitch the side borders to the quilt top using the same techniques used in Step 7.
- Measure the top and lower edges of the quilt top.
- Cut 4 borders the length of the top and lower edges.
- Cut and seam the batting as detailed for the side borders.
- Stitch the top and lower borders to the quilt top using the same techniques used in Step 7.

9 BIND THE QUILT

- Use your favorite method or refer to pages 120–121.

The Original Column Quilt: Double Size

Once you've made a lap quilt, take your new skill to a larger palette. By increasing the length and number of columns, this easy-to-piece design can be made into a double- or full-size bed quilt. The gradation of colors provides great visual impact.

FINISHED SIZE

- Approximately 80" × 96" (203.2cm × 243.8cm)

SUPPLIES

- 1½ yards (1.4m) Fabric A (red print) for 1 column, inner border and binding
- 2⅜ yards (2.2m) Fabric B (yellow) for 2 columns and outer borders
- ¾ yard (.7m) Fabric C (orange print) for 2 columns
- ¾ yard (.7m) Fabric D (green) for 2 columns
- ¾ yard (.7m) Fabric E (blue print) for 2 columns
- ¾ yard (.7m) Fabric F (aqua) for 2 columns
- 5½ yards (5m) backing fabric
- Batting for a double-size quilt
- Essential Quiltings Tools (see listing on page 110)

NOTE FROM NANCY

This quilt can easily be made into a queen- or king-size quilt. The queen-size quilt requires two more column units, and the king-size quilt requires four additional column units. The yardage listed under Fabrics A and B, which includes column units, binding and borders, will accommodate both larger-size quilts. For the backing, refer to pages 113–114 for creative ways to back large quilts using a combination of yardage and leftover fabric from making the column units.

Additional supplies needed for a queen-size quilt:

- ¾ yard (.7m) Fabric G for 2 columns
- Batting for a queen-size quilt

Additional supplies needed for a king-size quilt:

- ¾ yard (.7m) Fabric G for 2 columns
- ¾ yard (.7m) Fabric H for 2 columns
- Batting for a king-size quilt

Note: All seam allowances are ¼" (6mm) unless otherwise stated.

1 PREPARE AND CUT THE FABRICS

- Stabilize all fabrics well using spray starch or a starch alternative such as Mary Ellen's Best Press. See page 112.
- Fabric A (red print):
  - Cut six 2½" (6.4cm) crosswise strips.
  - Cut one 5" (12.7cm) crosswise strip.
  - Reserve the remaining fabric for the inner border and binding.
- Fabric B (yellow):
  - Cut nine 2½" (6.4cm) crosswise strips.
  - Cut two 5" (12.7cm) crosswise strips.
  - Reserve the remaining fabric for the outer border.
- Fabrics C, D, E, and F: Cut ten 2½" (6.4cm) crosswise strips.
  - Cut two 5" (12.7cm) crosswise strips.
- Organize the strips arranging them from Fabric A through Fabric F. Figure 1.
- A queen- or king-size quilt requires additional column units, Fabrics G and H.
  - Cut ten 2½" (6.4cm) crosswise strips and two 5" (12.7cm) crosswise strips from each of these fabrics.

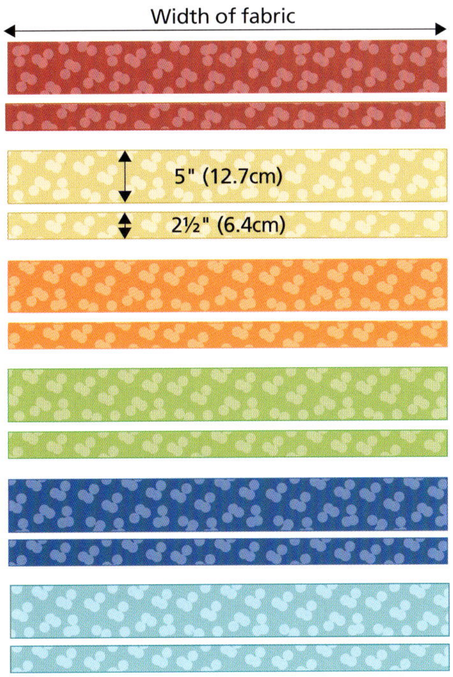

Figure 1

2 PREPARE THE COLUMN UNITS

For this quilt, you'll need 11 column units for double-size quilts, 13 for queen-size quilts, and 15 for king-size quilts.

- For each outer strip, seam the short ends of two 2½" (6.4cm) crosswise strips of the same fabric, right sides together.
- Since fabrics are not consistent in width, ranging from 41"–45" (104.1cm–114.3cm), trim all outer strips to the same length. The seamed strips measure approximately 82" (208.3cm).
- Press seams flat, then press them in 1 direction.
- Prepare 2 outer strips using Fabric A.
- Prepare 4 outer strips each of Fabrics B, C, D, E and F (and G and/or H if making a queen- or king-size quilt.)
- Transfer the remaining unsewn 2½" × 42" (6.4cm × 106.7cm) strips to the fabric grouping of the previous coloration. For example, the extra strips of B will be placed in the A grouping; the extra strips of C will be placed in the B grouping; the extra strips of A will be placed in the F grouping (or grouping G for a queen-size quilt or grouping H for a king-size quilt). Figure 2.
- Prepare the middle strip stratas. To do this, stitch the 5" (12.7cm) Fabric A strip to the 2½" (6.4cm) Fabric B strip, creating 1 strata. Figure 3.
- For the remaining fabrics, create 2 stratas for the middle strip, stitching the 5" (12.7cm) fabric strip to the 2½" (6.4cm) fabric strip.
- Subcut each strata into 2½" (6.4cm) sections. For Fabric A, 14 subcuts are needed. For all other fabrics, 28 subcuts are needed. Figure 4.
- For each middle strip of the column unit, stitch 14 subcuts together at the short ends, right sides together.
- Press the seams flat, then press them in 1 direction.

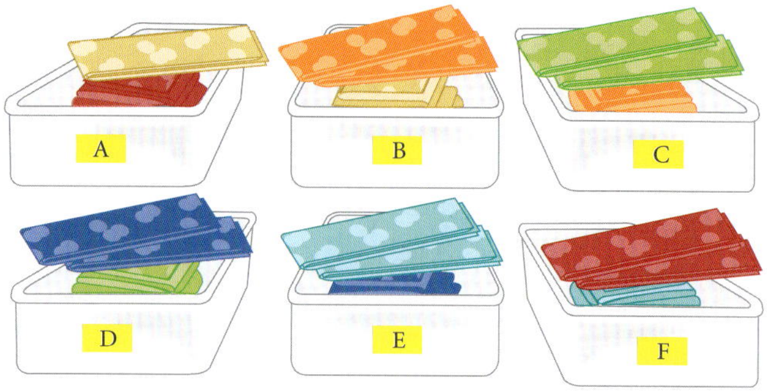

Figure 2

Figure 3

Figure 4

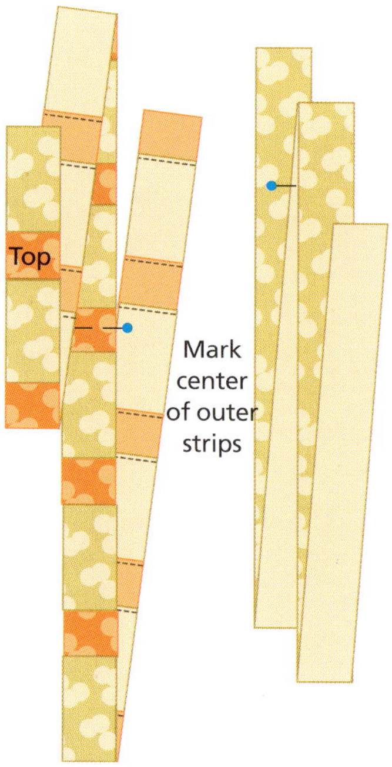

Figure 5

- For colors B, C, D, E, and F (also G and/or H for a queen- or king-size quilt), create 2 middle strips.
- Pin mark the column strips. To do this, place a pin at the center of the seventh square block in the middle strip. Count from the top of the pieced strip.
- Fold each outer strip in half and meet the short ends. Place a pin at the fold. Figure 5.
- Pin the middle strip to the 2 outer strips, right sides together. Be sure to match the pin marks. A portion of the middle strip will extend above and below the outer strips. Figure 6.
- Stitch the outer strips to the middle strip to create a column unit.
- Trim off the excess length of the middle section.
- Press the seams flat, then press them in 1 direction.

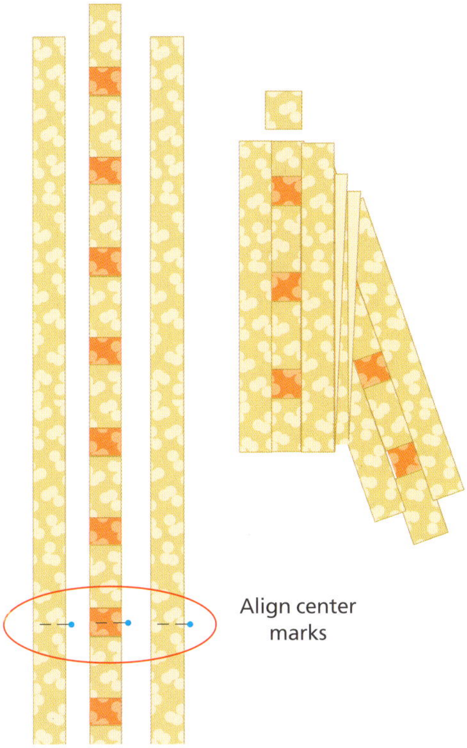

Figure 6

Figure 7

Figure 8

NOTE FROM NANCY

Since the column units are long, consider quarter marking each column unit. Fold lengthwise in half and then into quarters, placing a pin at each quarter mark. Match and pin the quarter marks prior to stitching the seams to ensure accuracy.

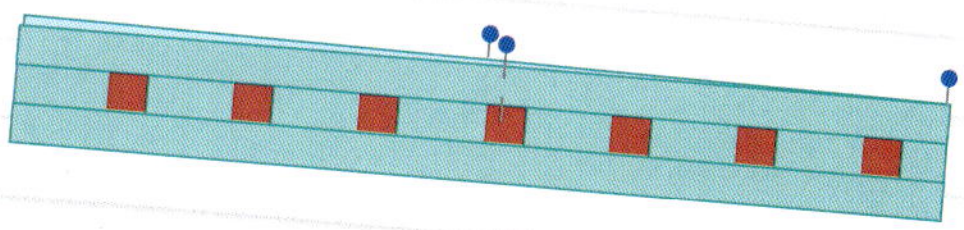

3 LAYOUT AND COMPLETE THE QUILT TOP

- Position the Fabric A column unit in the center.
- Position the column units on both sides of the center column unit in order, as shown in Figure 7.
- Stitch the column units, right sides together, making sure to position the strips so the squares align across the quilt top. Press seams flat, then press them in 1 direction. Figure 8.

4 CUT INNER BORDERS AND BINDING STRIPS

- For a double-size quilt: From the remaining Fabric A, cut the following.
  - Eight 1½" (3.8cm) crosswise strips for inner borders
  - Nine 2½" (6.4cm) crosswise strips for binding
- For a queen-size quilt: From the remaining Fabric A, cut the following.
  - Eight 1½" (3.8cm) crosswise strips for inner borders
  - Ten 2½" (6.4cm) crosswise strips for binding
- For a king-size quilt: From the remaining Fabric A, cut the following.
  - Nine 1½" (3.8cm) crosswise strips for inner borders
  - Ten 2½" (6.4cm) crosswise strips for binding

5 PREPARE AND ADD INNER BORDERS

- Stitch the short ends of inner border strips, right sides together. Press the seams flat, then press them open. Figure 9.
- Measure the side lengths of the quilt top.
- Cut 2 inner borders the length of the side measurement.
- Stitch the inner borders to the sides of the quilt top, right sides together. Press the seams flat, then press them toward the borders. Figure 10.

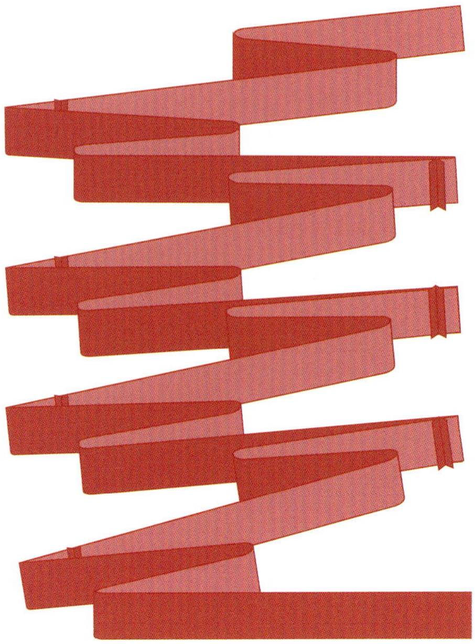

Figure 9

Figure 10

- Measure the length of the top and lower edges of the quilt top.
- Cut 2 inner borders the length of the top and lower edge measurements.
- Stitch the inner borders to the top and lower edges of the quilt top, right sides together. Press the seams flat, then press them toward the borders. Figure 11.

6 CUT OUTER BORDERS

- For a double-size quilt: From the remaining Fabric B, cut eight 6½" (16.5cm) crosswise strips.
- For a queen-size quilt: From the remaining Fabric B, cut nine 4½" (11.4cm) crosswise strips.
- For a king-size quilt: From the remaining Fabric B, cut ten 5½" (14.0cm) crosswise strips.

7 PREPARE AND ADD OUTER BORDERS

- Stitch the short ends of the outer border strips, right sides together. Press the seams flat, then open.
- Measure the side lengths of the quilt top.
- Cut 2 outer borders the length of the side measurement.
- Stitch the outer borders to the sides of the quilt top, right sides together. Press the seams flat, then toward the borders.
- Measure the length of the top and lower edges of the quilt top.
- Cut 2 outer borders the length of the top and lower edge measurement.
- Stitch the outer borders to the top and lower edges of the quilt top, right sides together. Press the seams flat, then press them toward the borders. Figure 12.

8 LAYER, QUILT AND BIND

- Use your favorite methods or refer to pages 114–121.
- Use Fabric A binding strips for the binding.

Figure 11

Figure 12

80" × 96" (203.2cm × 243.8cm)

CHAPTER THIRTEEN

Quilt to Give

The gift is in the giving! For those of us who sew and quilt, donating what we create gives us two gifts: the joy of creating and the satisfaction of helping others. This last chapter features instructions on how to sew a column quilt that can be made from a fabric stash, how to set up a modern-day quilting bee and how to give the quilts away.

Note: All seam allowances are ¼" (6mm) unless otherwise stated.

1 SORT FABRICS

Check out your fabric stash. When looking at my stash of fabric, my head was swimming. What a mess! Alas, I didn't think I had enough leftover fabrics to create an attractive quilt.

In the past, I might have left the stash just as I found it—unorganized. But I was determined to organize and cull my fabric stash to create an attractive, well-planned quilt that I could give away. Figure 1.

Sorting Tips

- Choose an inspirational fabric. Select several fabric prints that have a variety of colors.
- Gather solid-colored fabrics that coordinate or match with each print. Choose as many solids or mottled (subtle prints that appear as solid colors from a distance) fabrics as possible. The solid fabrics will be used for the outside strips of each column unit.
- Create several stacks of fabric. Place the inspirational fabric on top. Figure 2.
- Decide which fabric grouping will be the candidate for the Quilt to Give.
- Measure the solid fabrics to make certain there is enough yardage to create 1, 2 or more outside strips for the column unit. Each column unit requires 10" × 42" (25.4cm × 106.7cm) of fabric.
- Write the yardage on a note and attach it to the fabric. Later this notation will help you decide how many outside strips can be cut from the fabric. Figure 3.

NOTE FROM NANCY

Several years ago, I developed and wrote lessons on how to make a quilt from a fabric stash. Modifying the Original Column Quilt (page 90) by making a scrappy center strip and offering color options for the column units, I posted the lessons online in my blog (nancyzieman.com/blog).

The feedback from this project was extremely positive. It was then decided that this design would be an ideal community service project at the annual Quilt Expo (www.wiquiltexpo.com) held in Madison, Wisconsin. For three years and counting, this design, now called "Quilt to Give," has inspired quilting enthusiasts attending the expo to take time from attending classes or shopping the vendor mall to sew for others.

2 DECIDE ON A COLUMN OPTION

A column unit is made up of 3 parts: 2 outside strips and a patchy center strip. Figure 4. I've come up with 4 different column options.

- Two color Column Units: Alternate 2 colors of column units. Figure 5.
- Three-color Column Units: Alternate 3 colors of column units. Figure 6.
- Gradated Column Units: same as the Original Column Quilt, page 90. There is a single-

Figure 1

Figure 2

Figure 3

colored column unit in the middle of the quilt top with pairs of column units gradating outward on both sides. (This option does not work for a twin-size layout.) Figure 7.

- Varied Column Units: Each column unit is a different color. Figure 8.

3 DETERMINE YOUR QUILT SIZE

A twin-size quilt requires 10 column units.
A double-size quilt requires 11 column units.
A queen-size quilt requires 13 column units.
A king-size quilt requires 15 column units.

Figure 4

NOTE FROM NANCY

I chose the Gradated Column unit for my double-size Quilt to Give since I had more than seven solid colors of fabric to use as the outside strips. I didn't have enough yardage of the red and black fabrics, so I set aside those two fabric pieces—you'll soon see them in the patchy grouping. It may be necessary to buy one or two fabrics to create an attractive color combination. So, you'll just have to go shopping!

Figure 5

Figure 6

Figure 7

Figure 8

4 FILL OUT THE WORKSHEET

- For easy reference, fill out the Quilt to Give Worksheet (see pages 108–109). Figure 9.
- Check the size options and column color options. Color the Column Units Layout with colored pencils.

5 GATHER FABRICS FOR THE PATCHY CENTER STRIPS

- Move the solid fabrics not selected for the outer strips to the inspirational fabric pile.
- Gather more prints and solid fabrics that coordinate or match with the inspirational fabric. Short yardages can be used.

6 CUT OUTER COLUMN STRIPS

- Each column unit requires four 2½" (6.4cm) crosswise strips. Cut the fabrics selected for the column strips into 2½" (6.4cm) crosswise strips.
- Reference the worksheet to determine how many strips you need for each color.

7 CUT PATCHY STRIPS

- Vary the width of the patchy strip fabrics, ranging from 1½"–3½" (3.8cm 8.9cm).
- Cut 50 to 55 crosswise strips for a twin- or double-size quilt.
- Cut 60 to 65 crosswise strips for a queen-size quilt.
- Cut 70 to 75 crosswise strips for a king-size quilt.
- Cut the dark colors into narrow crosswise strips. Larger sections of dark colors can be too domineering while small sections of dark color add interest. Figure 10.
- Cut the inspirational print into crosswise strips for the patchy center strip. The print will not be that evident in the finished quilt, though it served a very important purpose of helping coordinate color and fabrics. Figure 11.

8 STITCH THE OUTSIDE COLUMNS

Each column is made up of 3 parts: 2 outside strips and a patchy center strip. Figure 12.

- Join 2 crosswise strips by stitching the short ends right sides together. To save time, chain stitch pairs of fabric strips. The length of each strip will be approximately 82" (208.3cm). Figure 13.
- After stitching, clip the threads between the stitching.
- Press the seams open or in 1 direction. Hang the strips over a hanger to keep them organized.

9 CREATE THE PATCHY CENTER STRIPS

- Pair up all the patchy strips. Choose contrasting colors and/or prints as pairs.
- Stitch 1 long edge of each strip pair. Figure 14. Chain stitch from 1 pair to the next. After stitching, clip the threads between the stitching.
- Press the seam allowances toward the darker color. Figure 15.

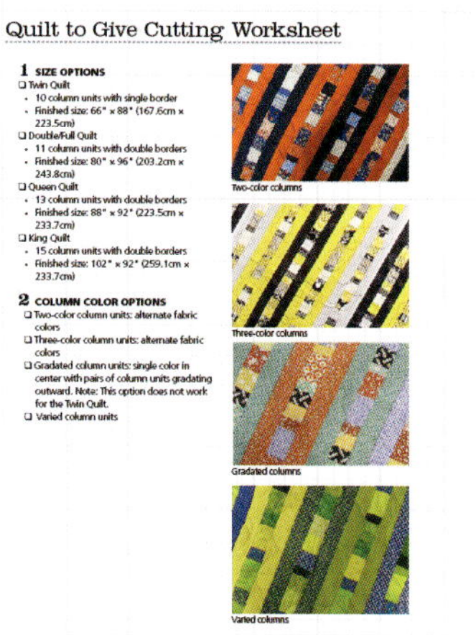
Quilt to Give Cutting Worksheet

1 SIZE OPTIONS
- ❑ Twin Quilt
  - 10 column units with single border
  - Finished size: 66" × 88" (167.6cm × 223.5cm)
- ❑ Double/Full Quilt
  - 11 column units with double borders
  - Finished size: 80" × 96" (203.2cm × 243.8cm)
- ❑ Queen Quilt
  - 13 column units with double borders
  - Finished size: 88" × 92" (223.5cm × 233.7cm)
- ❑ King Quilt
  - 15 column units with double borders
  - Finished size: 102" × 92" (259.1cm × 233.7cm)

2 COLUMN COLOR OPTIONS
- ❑ Two-color column units: alternate fabric colors
- ❑ Three-color column units: alternate fabric colors
- ❑ Gradated column units: single color in center with pairs of column units gradating outward. Note: This option does not work for the Twin Quilt.
- ❑ Varied column units

Two-color columns

Three-color columns

Gradated columns

Varied columns

Figure 9

Figure 10

Figure 11

- Stitch 2 pairs together. At this point, there are 4 strips in a strata. Create attractive color combinations. Figure 16.
- Repeat stitching strip sections together and adding an equal number of strips to each of the 4 stratas until all the patchy strips have been used.
- Measure the length of each strata. The combined length must equal 82" (208.3cm) or more. It may be necessary to add yet another pair of strips to 1 strata to achieve the needed length.
- Stack 2 strata sections. Straight cut the left edge. Subcut the stratas into 2½" (6.4cm) crosswise strips. Repeat for the remaining strata sections. Figure 17.
- Stack like subcuts. Figure 18.

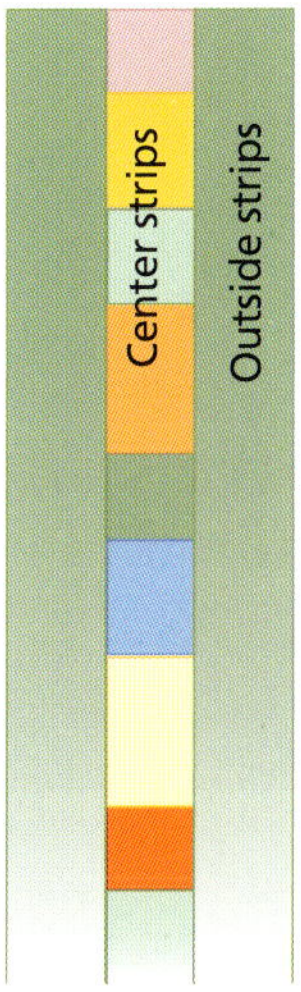

Figure 12

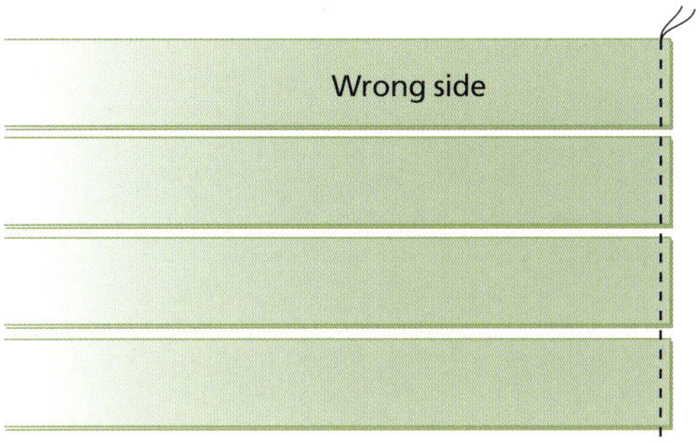

Figure 13

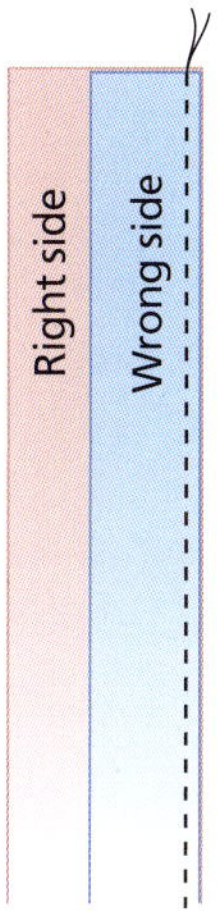

Figure 14

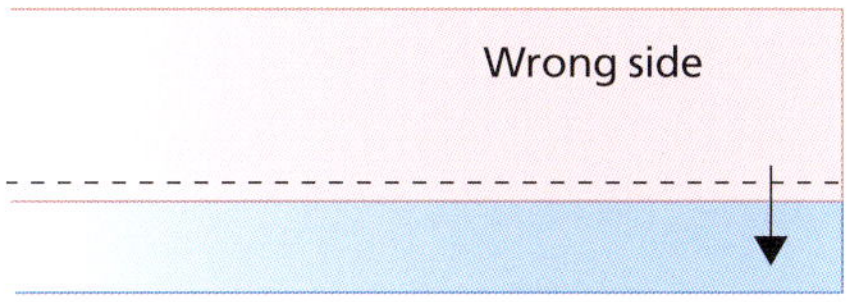

Figure 15

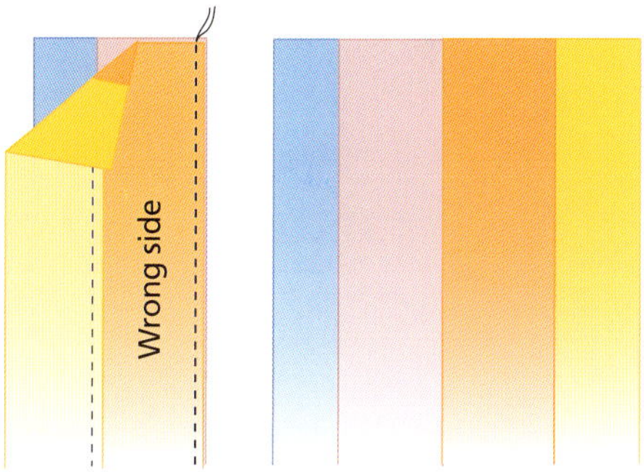

Figure 16

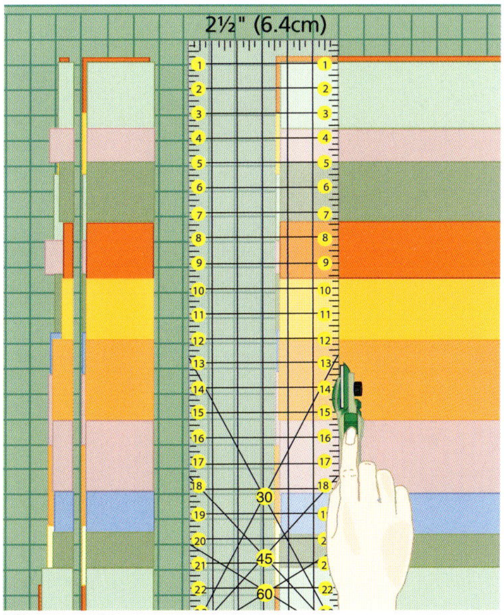

Figure 17

Figure 18

- The finished quilt features a different patchy strip in the middle of each column. To achieve a totally random look, select a subcut from each of the 4 stacks.
- Stitch the subcuts together, end to end. With each patchy section, switch the order of assembling the subcuts. For example, stitch the subcuts together in the following sequence: 1-2-3-4. Next time, stitch in a different order: 2-1-4-3. Rotate 1 or more of the subcuts 180° for another configuration. Figure 19.
- Lay out all the patchy strips on a cutting table or floor. Use safety pins to mark the top edge of each strip. Figure 20.

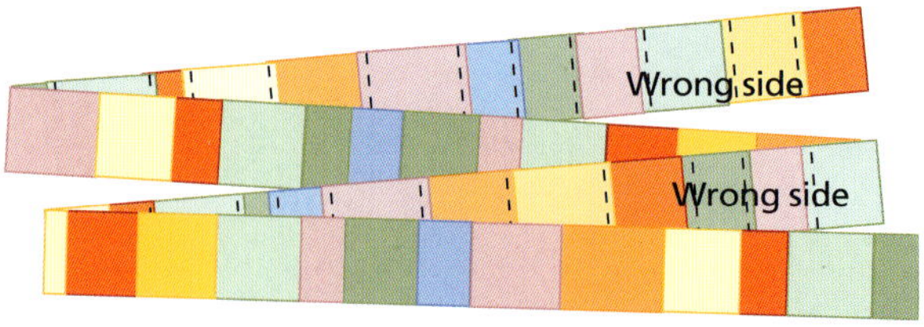

Figure 19

Figure 20

NOTE FROM NANCY

At our first Quilt to Give event, 5 yards (4.6m) of a striped fabric were donated. One look and I knew that we had a ready-made patchy center just by cutting 2½" (6.4cm) crosswise strips.

Striped fabrics make automatic patchy centers.

Quilt top made with striped fabric center strips.

10 CREATE THE COLUMN UNITS

- Lay out pairs of completed outside strips in the color sequence of your choosing. This example features a double-size bed quilt with 11 column units and the gradated layout option.
- Create a column unit by stitching a solid strip on each side of the patchy strip. Figure 21.
- Press the seam allowances toward the solid outside strips. Figure 22.
- Lay the column units on the floor or cutting table. Adjust the order of the column units to achieve an appealing layout. Figure 23.

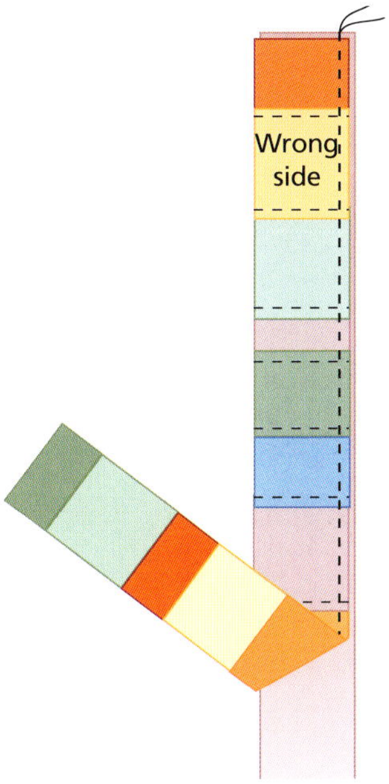

Figure 21

11 COMPLETE THE QUILT TOP

The remainder of the quilt top is completed the same way as the larger version of the Original Column Quilt, steps 3–8, starting on page 94.

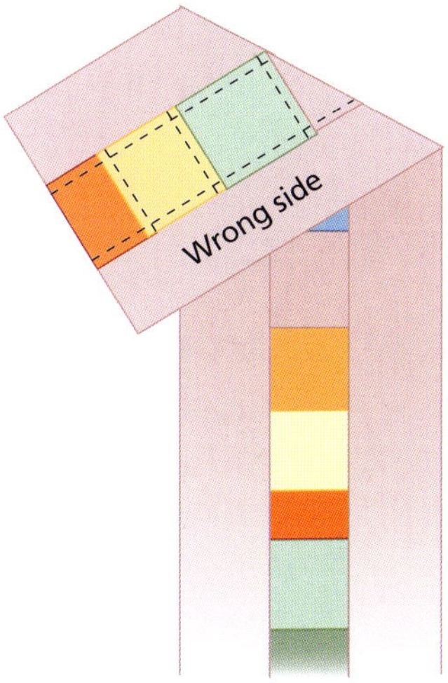

Figure 22

Figure 23

Plan a "Quilt to Give" Community Service Event

For three years and counting, the Quilt to Give pattern has served as the community service project at the annual Quilt Expo in Madison, Wisconsin. Close to twenty thousand people attend, with many attendees and volunteers taking time during the three-day event to donate fabric, cut strips, piece fabrics, and press and bind the finished quilts.

Other much smaller groups have come together to sew and cut quilts. Here are pointers on how groups—big or small—can work together to make full-size quilts for those in need.

1 CHOOSE PROJECT LEADERS

Theresa and Rachel are the leaders of the Quilt to Give group. They made a quilt in advance and knew the process well. Sharen and Judy precut several quilts and also helped at the event. We are grateful for all of our volunteers.

Theresa and Rachel

Sharen and Judy

2 REQUEST DONATIONS

As part of the Quilt Expo promotion, we sent out e-mails for fabric and batting requests. After the first year, we learned to request solids (needed for the outer column strips) and to note that fat quarters are too small for this project.

We also requested donations of finished quilts or quilt tops. The quilts could be of any design, but it was a special treat to receive finished Quilt to Give designs at the event.

3 REQUEST MACHINES AND OTHER DONATIONS

We have the good fortune of working with Baby Lock Sewing Machines. The dealer in Madison, M & R Sewing and Vacuum, donates the use of 10 sewing machines and a long arm machine during Quilt Expo. The Baby Lock Company

Nancy Zieman receives a donated Quilt to Give.

provides 2 educators to help with the project, including a long arm quilter. Three volunteers are scheduled every 3 hours to assist with the project.

For a smaller group, request fellow quilters to bring in their sewing machine. Not everyone needs a machine. Some people will be sorting fabrics, cutting strips and pressing.

Other donations to request include thread, scissors, needles, pins, rotary cutters, large cutting mats, long rulers, irons and ironing boards.

4 MAKE ADVANCED PREPARATIONS

For the Quilt to Give event, we have 2 or 3 quilts ready to sew. My staff and I sort fabrics and cut strips for the outer and patchy sections. For each quilt, a Quilt to Give Worksheet is filled out and fabrics are labeled. The fabrics are placed in a bin—1 bin per quilt.

5 SET UP THE EVENT

Our modern quilting bee is held at a convention center, so we are able to allocate a considerable amount of space for this event. Set up in the atrium, the Quilt to Give event enjoys great visibility as the attendees pass by the event on their way to classes.

Here's a summary of how the event is set up.

- Sign-In Station: We ask our attendees to sign a guest book. This is also where donated quilts are stacked to encourage admiration.
- Fabric Donation Station: Sort the donations by color to make the auditioning and selection process easier. Each year we have fabric left over to use as "seed" fabric for the next event.
- Sewing Machine Station: The number of machines needed depends upon the group size. Ten machines with notions (pins, thread nippers, and pincushion) are set on 8' (2.4m) tables.

Place all fabrics for one quilt in a bin.

The Sign-In Station is where we show off the finished quilts.

The Fabric Donation Station has all the fabric sorted by color.

At the Sewing Station, several machines are set up on each long table.

At the Pressing Station, volunteers press the donated fabric as well as the in-process quilts.

Cutting strips and patchy centers at the Cutting Station.

- Long Arm Quilting Station: Having a long arm quilting station with a professional quilter allows us to finish many quilts during the event. If a long arm quilting station is not an option, consider tying the quilt layers together.
- Cutting Stations: Designate 1 station for cutting strips and a second for squaring quilt tops.
- Pressing Stations: Sew-press-sew-press. We all know the value of pressing as we sew; the same rationale is applied at a modern quilting bee. Three pressing stations are set up at our event.

6 GIVE THE QUILT AWAY

The Quilt to Give project was inspired after seeing the devastation of the tornado that hit Joplin, Missouri, in 2011. It was only fitting that the quilts from our first event were sent to St. John's Mercy Medical Center in Joplin. Half of the quilts were given to hospital employees who lost their homes, and the other half were donated to individuals in the community.

With a little research, I know that you'll find recipients in your community who will appreciate receiving your Quilt to Give. Piece by piece, we can help stitch lives back together. You, too, will find that the gift is in the giving!

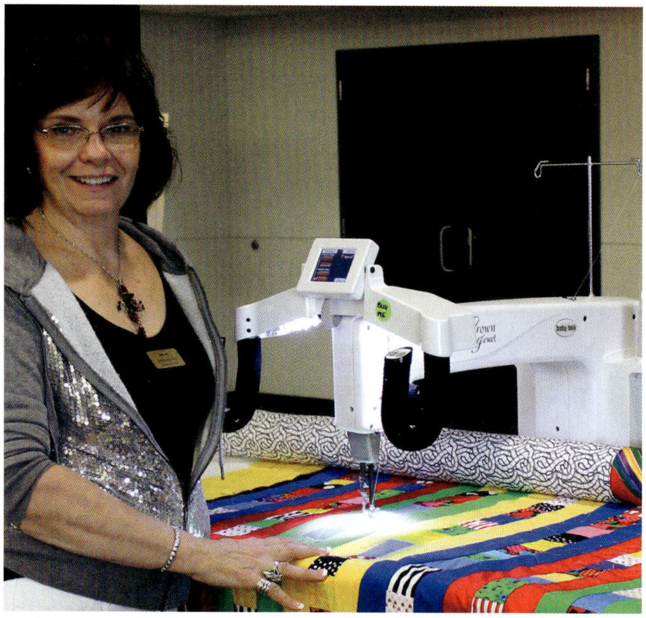

At the Long Arm Quilting Station, another beautiful quilt is loaded and ready for quilting.

Showing off a finished quilt.

Peter, our UPS driver, proudly handled our quilts.

Our volunteers know how to have fun!

Judy McCoy at St. John's Mercy Medical Center with a finished quilt.

Quilt to Give Cutting Worksheet

1 SIZE OPTIONS

❑ Twin Quilt
- 10 column units with single border
- Finished size: 66" × 88" (167.6cm × 223.5cm)

❑ Double/Full Quilt
- 11 column units with double borders
- Finished size: 80" × 96" (203.2cm × 243.8cm)

❑ Queen Quilt
- 13 column units with double borders
- Finished size: 88" × 92" (223.5cm × 233.7cm)

❑ King Quilt
- 15 column units with double borders
- Finished size: 102" × 92" (259.1cm × 233.7cm)

2 COLUMN COLOR OPTIONS

❑ Two-color column units: alternate fabric colors

❑ Three-color column units: alternate fabric colors

❑ Gradated column units: single color in center with pairs of column units gradating outward. Note: This option does not work for the Twin Quilt.

❑ Varied column units

Two-color columns

Three-color columns

Gradated columns

Varied columns

3 COLUMN UNITS LAYOUT

- Cut 4 crosswise strips for each column unit: 2½" × width of fabric (6.4cm × WOF).
- Use colored pencils to fill in the color of each column in the illustration below.

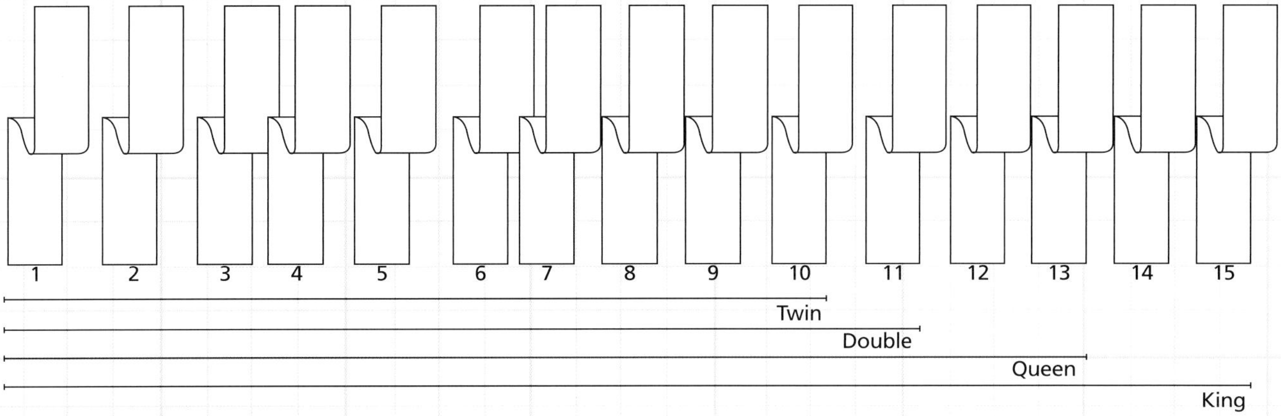

4 COLUMN STRIPS

Color	# of columns	# of crosswise strips needed
Example: Medium blue	3 × 4 = 12	
______________:	______	× 4 = ______
______________:	______	× 4 = ______
______________:	______	× 4 = ______
______________:	______	× 4 = ______
______________:	______	× 4 = ______
______________:	______	× 4 = ______
______________:	______	× 4 = ______
______________:	______	× 4 = ______
______________:	______	× 4 = ______

5 PATCHY CENTER STRIPS

Twin and Double: Cut 50–55 crosswise strips in a variety of widths from 1½" to 3½" (3.8cm to 8.9cm).
Queen: Cut 60–65 crosswise strips in a variety of widths from 1½" to 3½" (3.8m to 8.9cm).
King: Cut 70–75 crosswise strips in a variety of widths from 1½" to 3½" (3.8cm to 8.9cm).

6 BORDER STRIPS

Twin: Cut eight 3¼" (8.3cm) crosswise strips (requires ¾ yard [.7m] fabric)
Double: For the inner border, cut eight 1½" (3.8cm) crosswise strips (requires ⅓ yard [.3m] fabric).
- For the outer border, cut eight 6½" (16.5cm) crosswise strips (requires 1¼ yards [1.1m] fabric).

Queen: For the inner border, cut eight 1½" (3.8cm) crosswise strips (requires ⅓ yard [.3m] fabric).
- For the outer border, cut nine 4½" (11.4cm) crosswise strips (requires 1¼ yards [1.1m] fabric).

King: For the inner border, cut nine 1½" (3.8cm) crosswise strips (requires ⅜ yard [.3m] fabric).
- For the outer border, cut ten 5½" (14.0cm) crosswise strips (requires 1¼ yards [1.1m] fabric).

7 BINDING STRIPS

Twin: Cut eight 2½" (6.4cm) crosswise strips (requires ⅝ yard [.6m] fabric).
Double: Cut nine 2½" (6.4cm) crosswise strips (requires ¾ yard [.7m] fabric).
Queen: Cut ten 2½" (6.4cm) crosswise strips (requires ¾ yard [.7m] fabric).
King: Cut ten 2½" (6.4cm) crosswise strips (requires ¾ yard [.7m] fabric).

Column Quilt Basics

You need to know only a few rules, which are mainly guidelines, to create column designs. Here are the basics that will help you to quickly and easily make your column quilts.

Essential Quilting Tools

A plethora of quilting tools are available. These essentials will get you started on your first column quilt.

- **Rotary cutters:** A rotary cutter works much like a pizza cutter; it has a razor-sharp blade that cuts fabric with ease. Remember to retract the blade after each use to protect yourself and others. Rotary cutters come in a variety of sizes: 60mm, 45mm, 28mm and 18mm. The most common sizes used in quilting are 45mm and 60mm.
- **Cutting mat:** A cutting mat is a necessity when using a rotary cutter. Without the mat, the cutter would mar the tabletop. Mats of multiple sizes are available for convenience and efficiency. Look for a mat that is self-healing to assure longevity with normal use. The grid printed on the mat provides handy reference marks for measuring and cutting.
- **Rulers:** Rulers complete the cutting trio of rotary cutters, mat and rulers. The see-through acrylic ruler provides accurate measurements and a straight edge for cutting.

When shopping for a ruler, know that a 6" × 24" (15.2cm × 61.0cm) ruler is a convenient size for quilting. Another handy size is 4" × 12" (10.2cm × 30.5cm). Choose a laser-cut ruler that is marked in ⅛" (3mm) increments for the greatest cutting accuracy. Look for

Rotary cutter

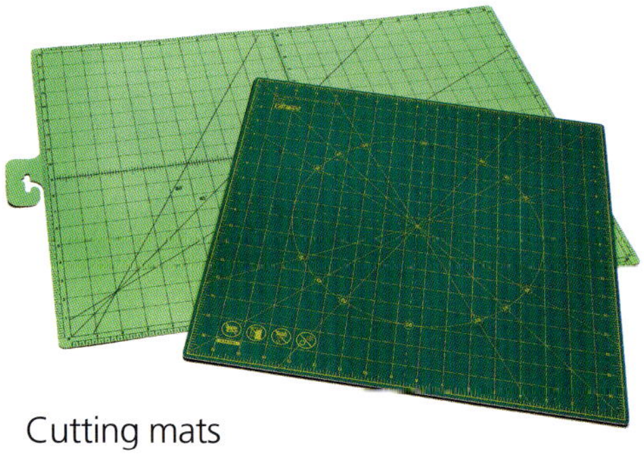

Cutting mats

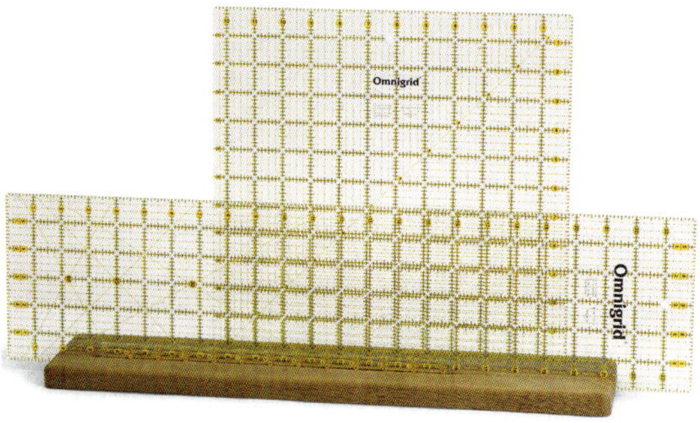

Rulers

NOTE FROM NANCY

The 18" × 24" (45.7cm × 61.0cm) mat is the most commonly used size. Many quilters have numerous mats.

two-color rulers (black/yellow or black/green) that can be used effectively on light or dark colored fabrics.

- **Shears/Scissors:** Shears have one large hole for fingers and a smaller hole for your thumb. The blades of shears can be either straight or bent and are more than 6" (15.2cm) long. A scissors has two finger holes the same size, and the blades are less than 6" long (15.2cm). My advice is to purchase the best quality shears or scissors you can afford. Your hands will definitely thank you!
- **Thread:** For machine piecing, use cotton or cotton-covered polyester thread. For machine quilting, use matching cotton thread or monofilament thread that is thin and soft.
- **Machine quilting needles:** Machine quilting needles are recommended over the traditional universal needle since these needles have a specially tapered ultrasharp point and extra-stiff shaft to provide better stitching through multiple layers of fabric.
- **Patchwork foot:** Attach this to the sewing machine to help stitch accurate ¼" (6mm) seams. You can use a patchwork foot or a Little Foot. The right side of the foot is exactly ¼" (6mm) wide. Position the right edge of the foot along the cut edges of the fabric for uniform seams every time.
- **Darning or quilting foot:** Use for free-motion quilting (page 118). The foot has a shorter shank (height), allowing you to easily guide the fabric while stitching a design.

Shears/scissors

Thread

Machine quilting needle

Universal needle

NOTE FROM NANCY

You might think it's odd not to reference hand sewing needles. Since the quilts in this book are speedy to sew, the only reference to hand stitching is the option to hand stitch the binding to the back of the quilt. Save hand stitching for another quilt design!

Cutting Fabric Strips

What makes column quilts quick to create is the use of columns instead of blocks. The rotary cutting trio—rotary cutter, mat and ruler—speed up the column-cutting process. Here are simple steps to cutting crosswise strips for column quilts.

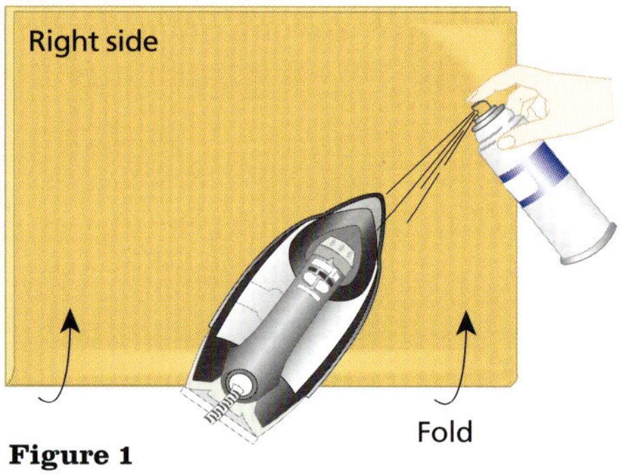

Figure 1

1 STARCH AND IRON

- Meet the selvage edges of the fabric. Apply spray starch or starch alternative, such as Mary Ellen's Best Press, on the whole cut of fabric. Press with an iron. The spray, combined with pressing, adds crispness to the fabric, making it easier to cut. Figure 1.

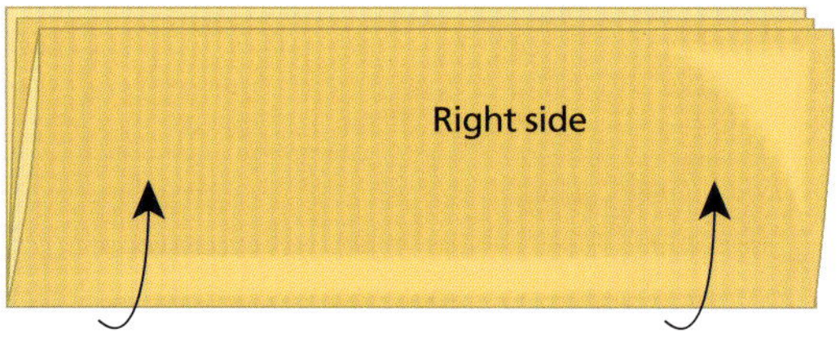

Figure 2

2 FOLD THE FABRIC

- After pressing, fold the fabric in half again and bring the fold to the selvages. You now have 4 layers of fabric. Figure 2.

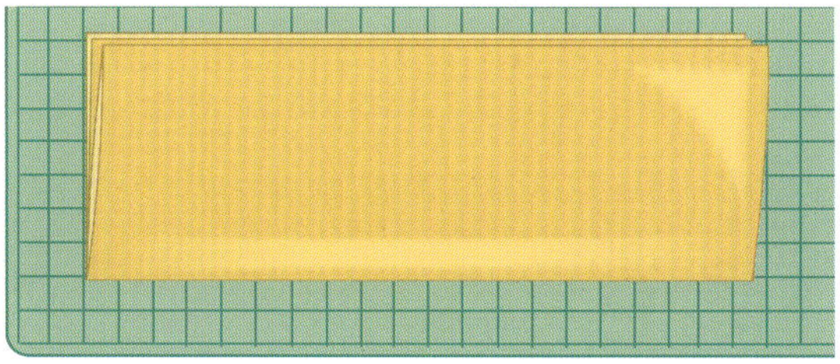
Figure 3

3 ALIGN THE FABRIC

- Place the fabric on a rotary cutting mat. Align the fold along 1 of the horizontal lines at the lower edge of the mat. Figure 3.

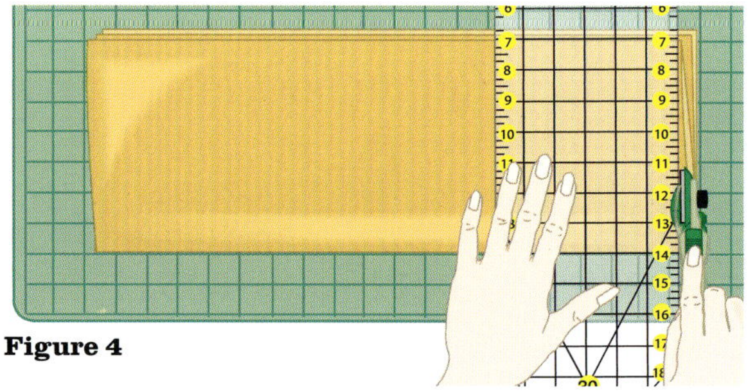
Figure 4

4 TRIM EXCESS FABRIC

- Position a ruler on the fabric perpendicular to the fold so it forms a right angle. Straighten the fabric edges and use the rotary cutter to trim away any excess fabric.
- For greatest accuracy, I prefer to have the majority of the fabric to the left of the ruler when I make that first cut. Firmly hold the ruler in position with your left hand and cut with your right. Before cutting the strips, carefully rotate the mat so the trimmed edge of the fabric is on the left. Figure 4.

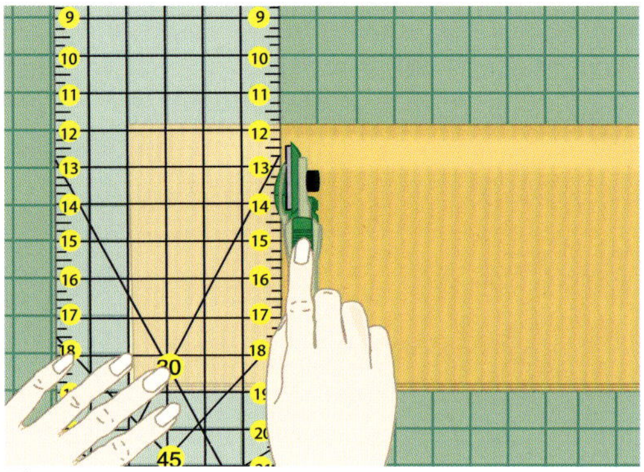
Figure 5

5 CUT CROSSWISE STRIPS

- Following the instructions given in your specific projects, cut fabric into crosswise strips. To do this, align 1 of the ruler's horizontal lines with the fabric fold. Working from the straightened edge, place the line that corresponds to the desired strip width along the straightened edge of the fabric. Figure 5.

Determining Backing Fabric Yardage

The term backing fabric is self-explanatory; but achieving the correct backing size requires a few guidelines. Here are the simple rules to follow when purchasing and piecing the backing fabric.

First measure the quilt top. Add 4"–6" (10.2cm–15.2cm) to the length and width. Doing so will make the backing fabric 2"–3" (5.1cm–7.6cm) larger than the quilt top on all four sides.

Next purchase and stitch the backing fabric. For a crib-size quilt, purchase one length of 42"-wide (106.7cm) fabric the length needed for backing.

For a twin or double quilt, purchase 42"-wide (106.7cm) fabric twice the length needed for backing. Cut the fabric in half, creating two lengths.

Cut one of the lengths in half lengthwise, making two sections. If this width, approximately 80" (203.2cm), is too wide for the backing, trim off the extra fabric prior to cutting it into two sections.

Join the sections with a ¼" (6mm) seam, right sides together. Place the 42" (106.7cm) fabric in the center and the 21" (53.3cm) sections on either side.

For a queen- or king-size quilt, purchase one length of 108"–120"-wide (274.3cm–304.8cm) backing fabric. If only 42"-wide (106.7cm) fabric is available, you don't have to purchase a third length of fabric to accommodate that width. Instead stitch a quilt column down the center from extra quilt top fabric.

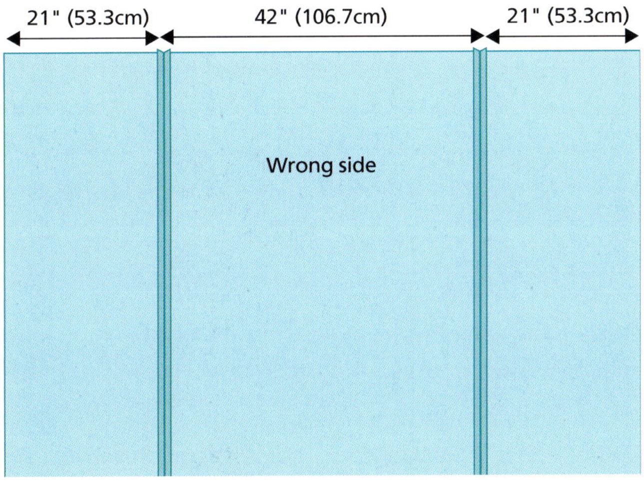

Seams in the backing of a twin- or double-size quilt

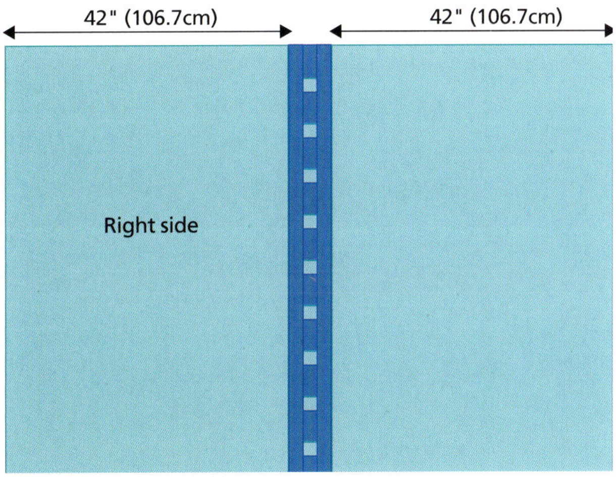

Seams in the backing of a queen- or king-size quilt

QUILT SIZE GUIDELINES

For reference, listed are size guidelines for quilt tops. Note that the actual quilt size can vary; there is not a hard and fast rule.

	Width	Length
Baby	36"–45" (91.4cm–114.3cm)	45"–54" (114.3cm–137.2cm)
Crib	42"–48" (106.7cm–121.9cm)	54"–60" (137.2cm–152.4cm)
Lap/Nap	54"–60" (137.2cm–152.4cm)	68"–76" (172.7cm–193.0cm)
Twin	56"–64" (142.2cm–162.6cm)	84"–100" (213.4cm–254.0cm)
Double/ Full	70"–80" (177.8cm–203.2cm)	84"–100" (213.4cm–254.0cm)
Queen	76"–84" (193.0cm–213.4cm)	90"–104" (228.6cm–264.2cm)
King	92"–100" (233.7cm–254.0cm)	90"–105" (228.6cm–266.7cm)

Cotton batt

Cotton/polyester batt

Wool batt

Batting Choices

Batting gives a quilt loft or thickness. Low-loft or thin batting is ideal for hand and machine quilting. High-loft batting is primarily used for tied quilts or comforters. The thicker the batting, the more difficult it is to quilt by machine. Whatever thickness you plan to use, choose a good-quality batting with an even loft. Many battings can be purchased in white or black.

Cotton batts

- Are lightweight, soft, and drape well
- Have low loft
- Are easy to quilt by machine
- Are a good choice for beginning quilters
- Are reasonably priced

Cotton/polyester blend batts

- Offer the ease of quilting by hand or machine, plus have a more traditional appearance
- Are less likely to beard
- Are warmer and heavier than polyester batting with the same loft
- Are reasonably priced

Wool batts

- Are warm and light
- Drape well and are easy to machine or hand quilt
- Have a slight tendency to beard
- Are more costly
- Must be dry-cleaned to prevent shrinkage and matting

Silk batts

- Drape well
- Can be sticky to stitch through
- May beard through cotton fabrics
- Are warm and lightweight
- Are more costly
- Should be dry-cleaned or delicately washed according to manufacturer's instructions

NOTE FROM NANCY

A professional long arm quilter quilted all of the large quilts in this book. Long arm quilters generally request wider/longer backing fabric, often 8" (20.3cm) to 12" (30.5cm) in both length and width, to accommodate the "leaders" on the quilt frame. Check with your long arm quilting professional for her/his preference.

SCRAPPY BACKING

Almost all of the quilts featured in this book have a scrappy backing fabric. That means that remaining fabrics and leftover sections of the columns were pieced together to create the needed length and width. Piecing the backing fabric can be as creative as making the quilt top.

Piecing the Batting

If you've made several quilts, chances are you have several leftover sections of the same batting. Here are the details on how to piece together odd-shaped sections to create a usable batt.

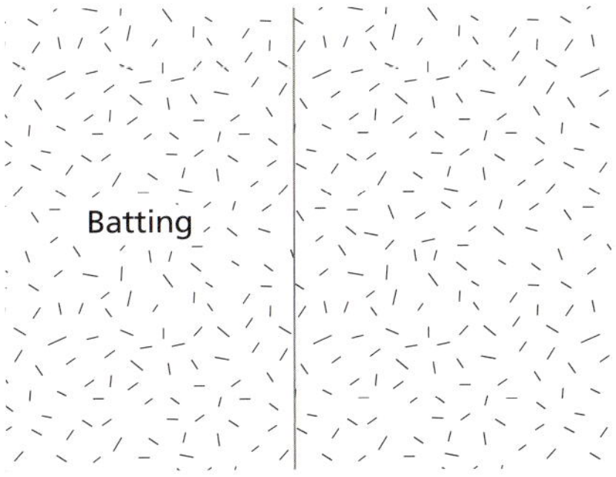

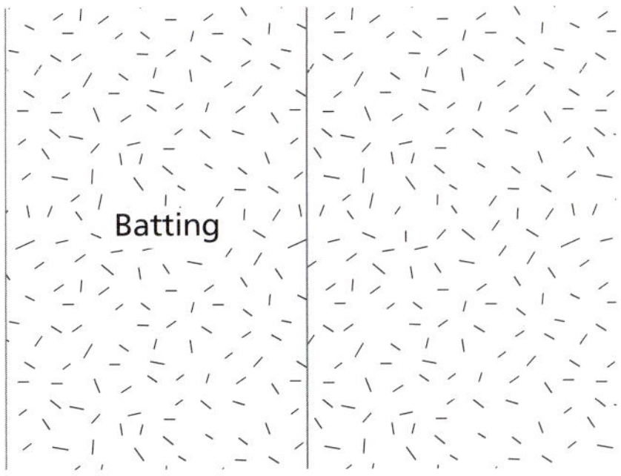

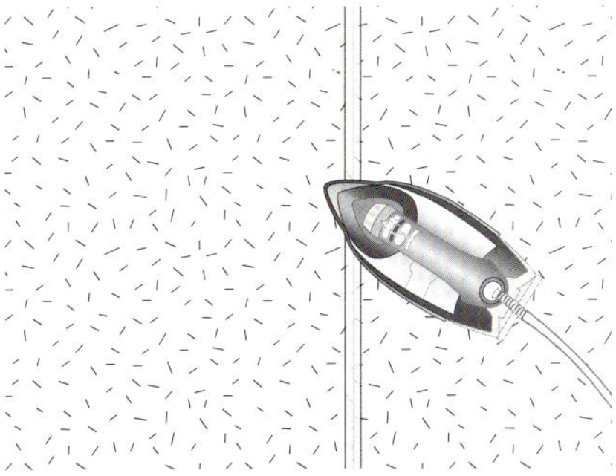

1 STACK BATTING

- Stack the 2 pieces of batting. Edges do not need to meet precisely; they will be trimmed to match.

2 CUT BATTING

- Use a rotary cutter and mat to cut through both layers.

3 SEAM TOGETHER

- Remove the trimmed remnants. Open the 2 cut sections and place them side by side, aligning the edges. Seam the sections together with a lightweight fusible tricot tape, such as Pellon's Batting Tape.

Pinning the Quilt Sandwich Together

You'll need a large, flat surface for pinning the quilt sandwich together. I often work on my ping-pong table. Its convenient height makes it a great surface for layering and pinning the fabrics.

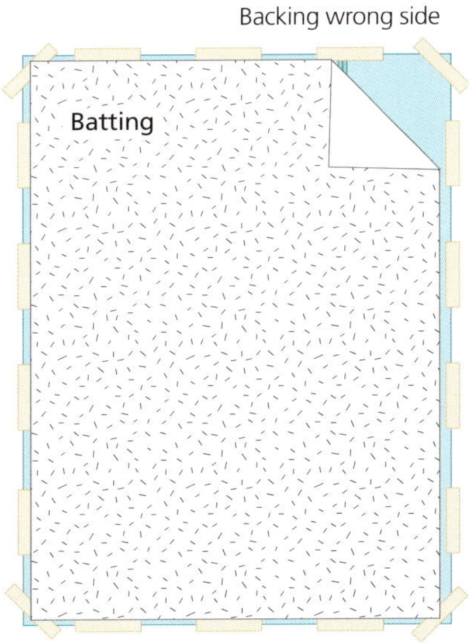

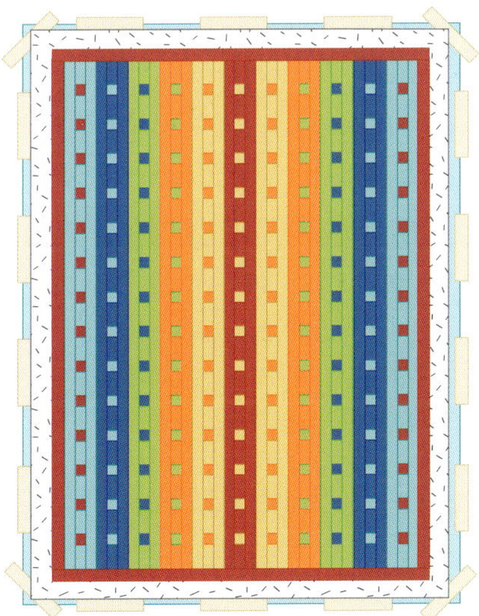

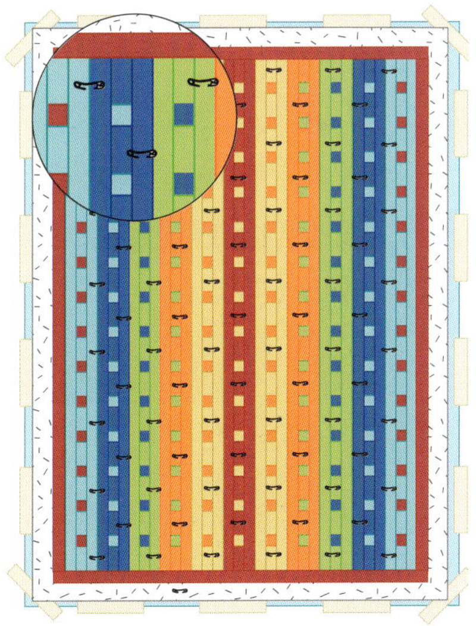

1 ARRANGE BATTING

- Place the backing fabric, wrong side up, on the surface. Secure the backing to the surface with masking tape. Center and smooth the batting over the backing.

2 CENTER TOP

- Center the quilt top, right side up, over the batting. Take time to smooth the layers so both are flat and without bubbles or puckers.

3 PIN LAYERS

- Pin the layers using curved basting pins. Begin —in the center, working toward the outer edges. Place pins a fist width apart, approximately 3"–4" (7.6cm–10.2cm). Avoid seams.

Fusing the Quilt Sandwich Together

Instead of pinning the layers of the sandwich together, you may choose to fuse them together. Here's the process for both small and large quilts.

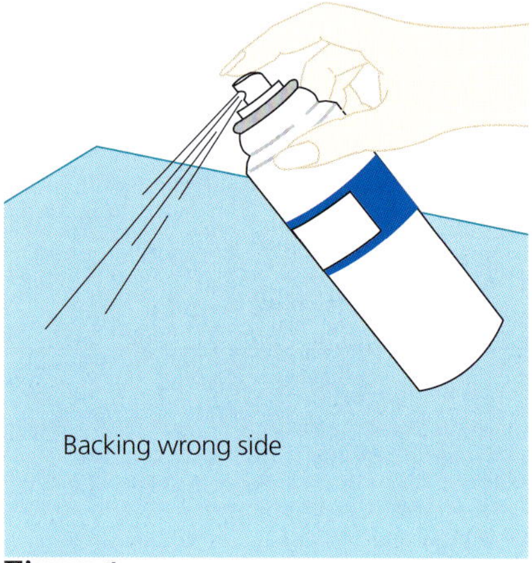

Figure 1

Figure 2

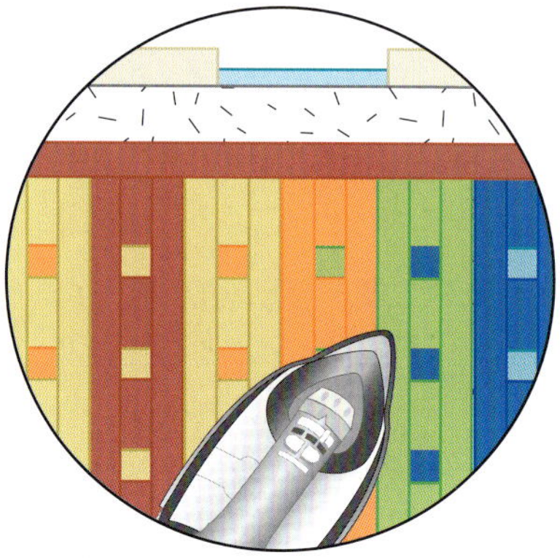

Figure 3

Small Projects

1 USE BASTING SPRAY

- For small projects, use quilt-basting spray, such as KK2000. Lightly spray the backing and apply the batting. Then spray the batting and apply the quilt top. Figure 1.

Large Projects

1 APPLY FUSIBLE WEB

- Fuse ½"-wide (1.3cm) strips of paper-backed fusible web, such as Pellon EZ-Steam II, to the wrong side of the backing and quilt top at 3"–4" (7.6cm–10.2cm) intervals before layering. Figure 2

2 REMOVE BACKING AND PRESS

- Remove the paper backing from the fusible web. Layer the quilt sandwich and press the layers together. Figure 3.

Rolling the Quilt Sandwich to Prepare for Stitching

If you'll be quilting your quilt on your home sewing machine, you'll need to roll the quilt so it will fit through the throat of the machine.

Roll the fabric from the side to the center. Secure the rolls with quilt clips or bicycle clips (clips worn around pant legs to keep the pants from getting stuck in the bicycle chain) to keep the quilt contained.

After quilting the open area (instructions given in the next section), reroll the quilt to expose a new section of the quilt.

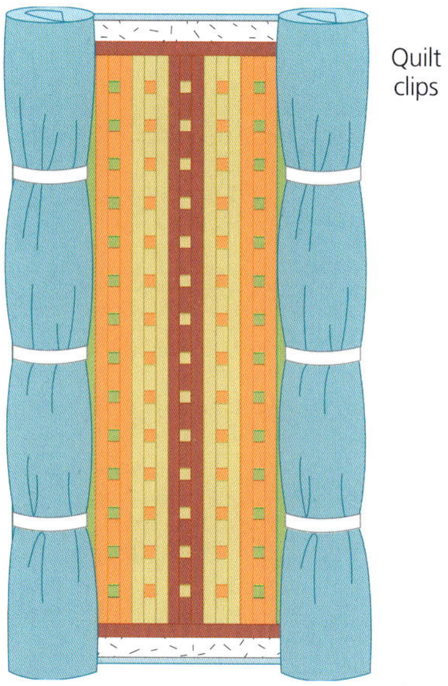

Quilt sandwich rolled and ready for machine quilting.

Quilting

For column quilts, you have several quilting options to consider. Among them are hand quilting, tying and various methods of machine quilting. Here are the details on a few.

Stitch in the Ditch

To stitch in the ditch references stitching in the "well" of the seam. This is an ideal way to quilt any of the column quilt designs.

1 PREPARE YOUR MACHINE

Set the sewing machine for a medium stitch length.

- Thread the top of the machine with cotton thread matched to the fabric. Or use monofilament thread, which is available in clear or smoke colorations and blends with a wide variety of fabric colorations, making thread changes unnecessary.
- Insert a new machine-quilting needle, size 80 or 90. Adjust the machine to stop with the needle in the "down" position.
- Attach a walking foot to feed the fabric evenly. It is important to prevent the layers of the quilt sandwich from shifting, and the walking foot helps feed all the layers through the machine smoothly and evenly.

2 STITCH IN THE DITCH

- Stitch in the ditch along each column in the well of the seam. Start in the center of the quilt and work toward the sides. Figure 1.

3 ALTERNATE DIRECTIONS

- Alternate the stitching directions with each row. Stitch from the top to the lower edge along one column. Then stitch the next row from the lower edge to the top of the next column. Figure 2

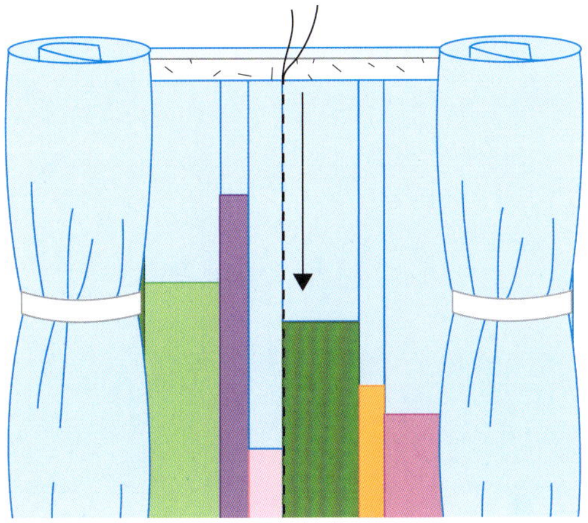

Figure 1

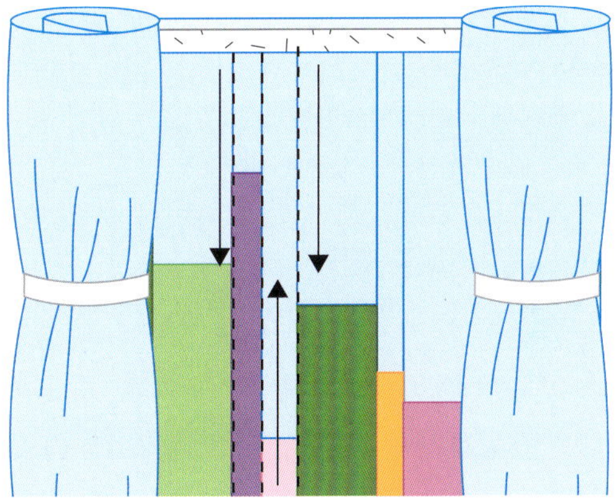

Figure 2

NOTE FROM NANCY

It is important to alternate stitching directions to prevent the quilt from becoming askew. This alternating method of stitching magically keeps the quilt square.

Stippling

Free-motion quilting or stippling is another way to quilt the layers of your column quilt. Likened to ice skating, the stitching pattern is free-flowing and graceful. You, rather than the machine, control how the fabric feeds through the machine.

1 ATTACH QUILTING FOOT

- Lower the feed dogs of your machine. Attach a quilting foot such as a darning/ quilting foot or a Big Foot. Many of these feet are clear, so you can easily see where you're stitching. The quilting foot glides above the quilt surface, allowing you to easily manipulate the fabric.

2 PREPARE YOUR MACHINE

- Set the machine for a straight stitch. You don't need to adjust the stitch length since the feed dogs are dropped and you control the stitching.
- Choose a cotton thread that matches your fabric. Or use monofilament thread, which is available in clear or smoke colorations.
- Insert a new machine-quilting needle, size 80 or 90. Adjust the machine to stop with the needle in the "down" position.

3 BEGIN QUILTING

- To guide the fabric, position your hands on both sides of the needle. Press the foot pedal at a fast speed while moving the fabric at a slow speed. Gently move the fabric to produce even stitches. Figure 1.

4 QUILT FREE-FORM DESIGN

- Make "puzzle piece" ends (left), tiny lightbulb shapes (middle) or any free-form design (right) you prefer. Figure 2.

Close up of stippling technique.

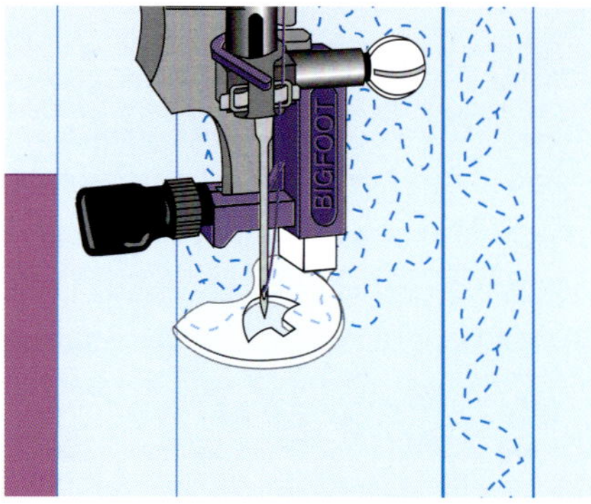

Figure 1

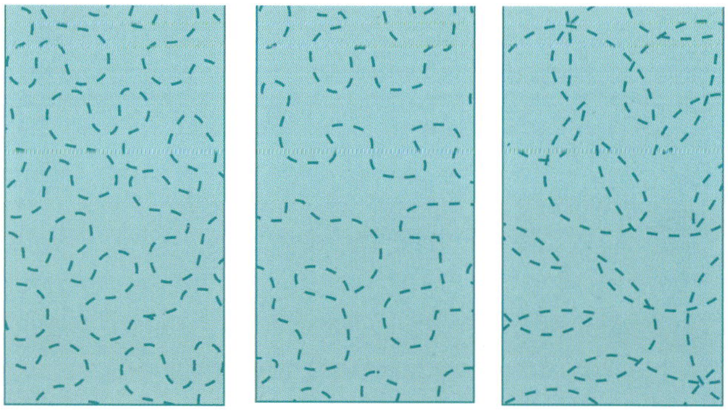

Figure 2

NOTE FROM NANCY

Have fun stippling! Cast aside any rules you have read: It's okay to cross stitches! I do recommend practicing your stippling on a sample fabric sandwich to get the feel of stippling before trying it on your column quilt.

Tying the Layers

Tying the layers of a column quilt is a great choice when you are using thick batting or when you would like to finish the quilting process as quickly as possible. Ask the help of friends and enjoy the camaraderie of a quilting social.

1 THREAD THE NEEDLE

- Select 12 wt. or thicker perle cotton thread. Use a long needle with an eye large enough for inserting 12 wt. thread.

2 TIE THE QUILT

- Tie the quilt layers together along the seam line. Place double knots a fist width apart, approximately 3"–4" (7.6cm–10.2cm). Figure 1.

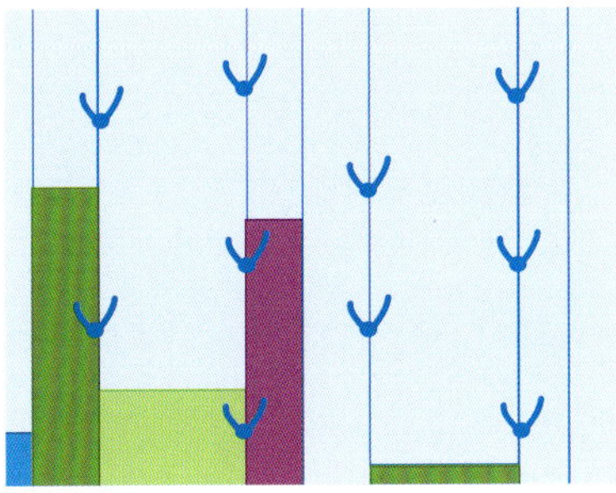

Figure 1

Attaching a Rod Pocket

A rod pocket is one of several ways to hang a column wall quilt. Although there are many different methods of making a rod pocket, this is my favorite. It's easy and fast to construct.

1 CUT AND FINISH THE EDGES

Cut a rod pocket from leftover fabric from the quilt top or backing.

- Make it 8" (20.3cm) wide and 2" (5.1cm) narrower than the width of the top of your wall hanging.
- Clean finish the 8" (20.3cm) edges of the rod pocket strip by turning under ¼" (6mm) on each edge twice. Press and stitch. Figure 1.

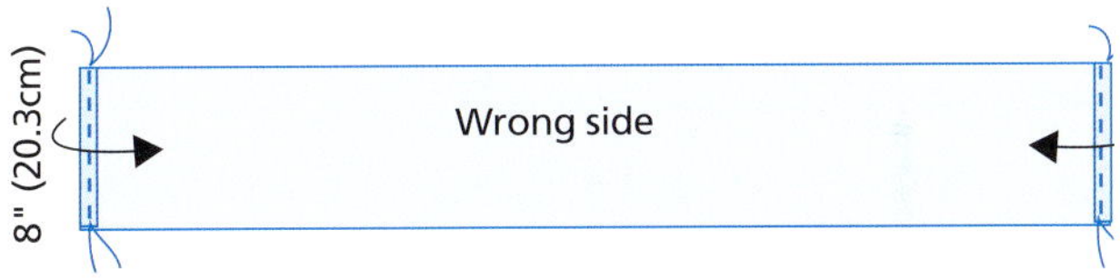

Figure 1

2 PRESS THE POCKET

- Press the rod pocket in half lengthwise, wrong sides together, meeting the cut edges. Figure 2.

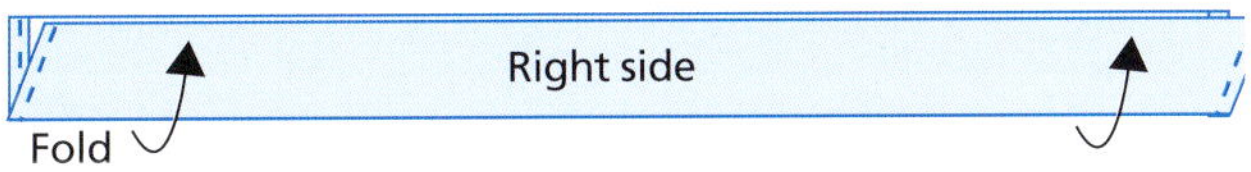

Figure 2

3 CENTER AND BASTE THE POCKET

- Center the rod pocket on the back of the wall hanging and align the top cut edges. Baste to the top edge of the quilt. Figure 3.

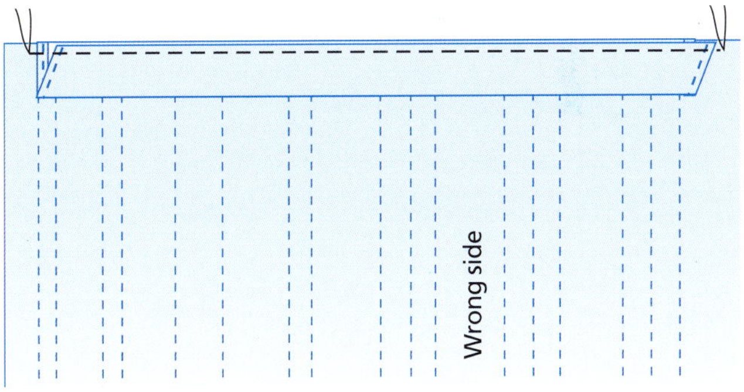

Figure 3

4 BIND POCKET IN PLACE

- Bind the edges (page 120). After the binding is attached, roll back the folded edge of the rod pocket to expose ½" (1.3cm) of the back of the rod pocket. The fold in the fabric will accommodate the width of the rod.
- Finger press along the new fold. Pin the finger-pressed fold to the backing fabric. Hand stitch along the pinned fold, catching only a single layer of the fabric. Figure 4.

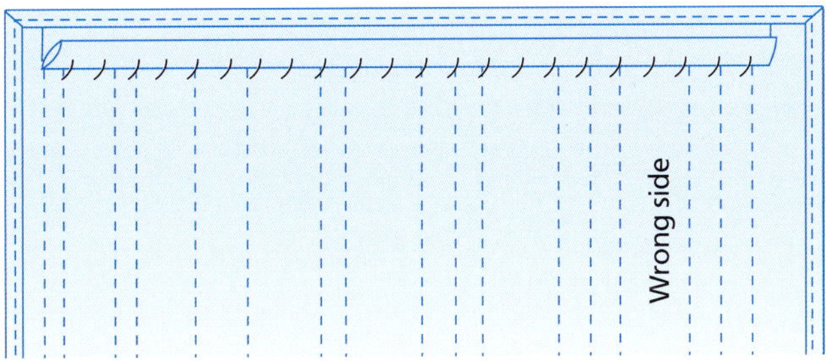

Figure 4

Binding

Undoubtedly, the job of binding a quilt lacks drama. Yet without the finished edge, your quilt just isn't finished! Use these tried-and-true techniques for binding your column quilts.

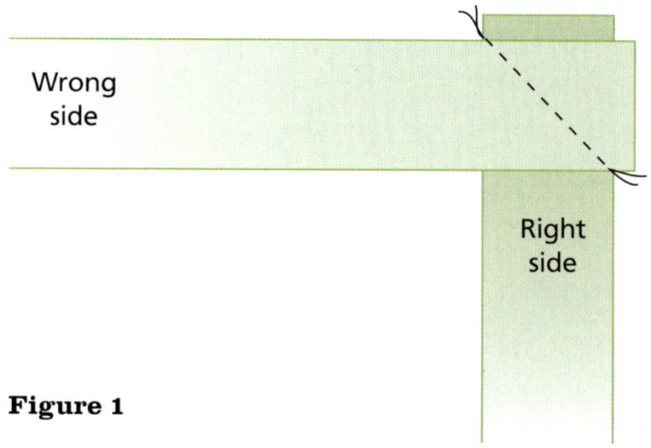

Figure 1

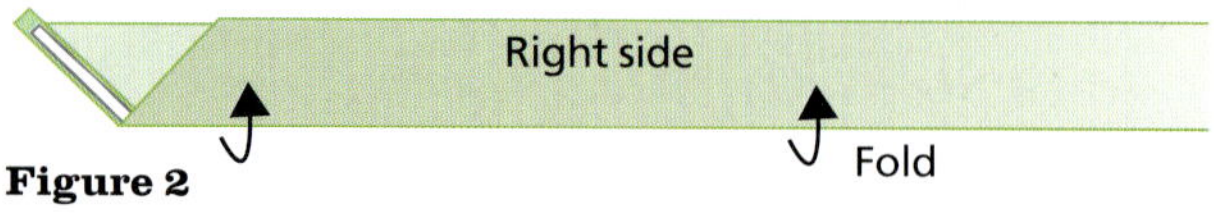

Figure 2

1 CUT CROSSWISE STRIPS

- Cut 2¼" (5.7cm) or 2½" (6.4cm) crosswise strips.
  - Use 2¼" (5.7cm) if you will stitch the last step of binding by hand or 2½" (6.4cm) crosswise strips if you will complete the entire binding by machine.
- Seam the short ends of the strips, right sides together, using a diagonal seam to minimize bulk. Figure 1.

2 APPLY FUSIBLE WEB

- Cut 1 end of the binding with a 45° angle.
- Fold in a generous ¼" (6mm) at the beginning angled edge.
- Press a ¼" (6mm) strip of paper-backed fusible web to the folded-under angled edge. Leave the paper backing in place.
- Fold the binding in half, wrong sides together, meeting the lengthwise edges. Press. Figure 2.

3 MARK THE CORNERS

- Place a mark on the quilt top ¼" (6mm) from each corner. Figure 3.

Figure 3

4 SEW TO FIRST CORNER

Use a ¼" (6mm) quilting foot or a patchwork foot.

- Meet the raw edges of the binding to the quilt top, right sides together. Start in the center of one edge with the beginning angled edge.
- Stitch the binding to the quilt with a ¼" (6mm) seam. Start stitching 4" (10.2cm) from the beginning angled edge.
- Stop stitching at the mark, with the needle in the fabric to lock the stitches. Cut the threads. Raise the presser foot. Figure 4.

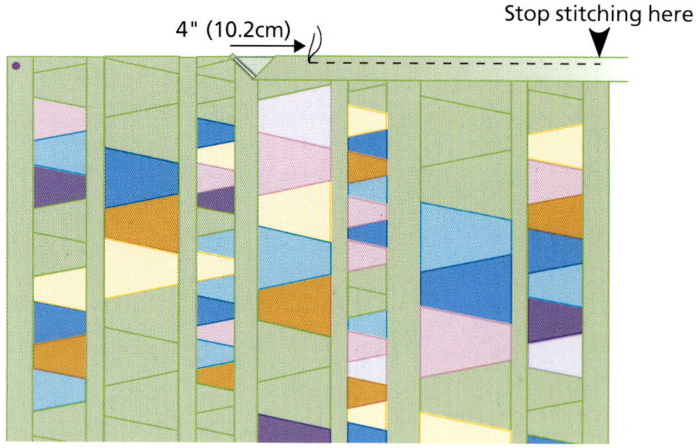

Figure 4

5 BIND AROUND THE CORNER

- Fold the binding up at a 45° angle. Align the cut edge of the binding with the cut edge of the quilt. Figure 5.
- Fold the binding down. Match the binding fold to the top edge of the quilt and match the binding cut edge to the quilt side edges.
- Lower the presser foot. Starting at the fold, stitch a ¼" (6mm) seam down the side, stopping at the next corner mark. Figure 6.

6 CONTINUE BINDING

Repeat at the remaining corners.

- When the binding reaches the starting point, unfold the binding; trim the excess.
- Remove the paper from the strip of paper-backed fusible web.
- Tuck the free end inside the beginning of the binding so it lays smooth.
- Press to fuse the binding ends together. Stitch the remaining seam. Figure 7.

7 PRESS BINDING AND PIN TO WRONG SIDE

- Press the binding away from the quilt top.
- Wrap the binding to the wrong side, covering the stitching line and tucking in the corners to form miters. Pin in place. Figure 8.

8 STITCH BINDING IN PLACE

- Secure the binding by stitching in the ditch (sewing in the well of the seam), from the right side of the quilt top (left, below). Or hand stitch the binding on the back side of the quilt (right, below). FIgure 9.

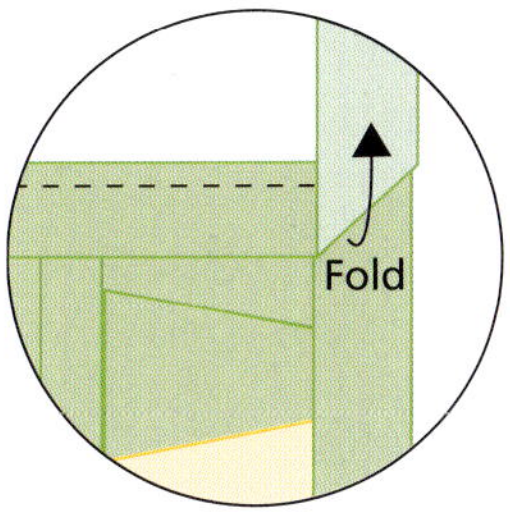

Figure 5

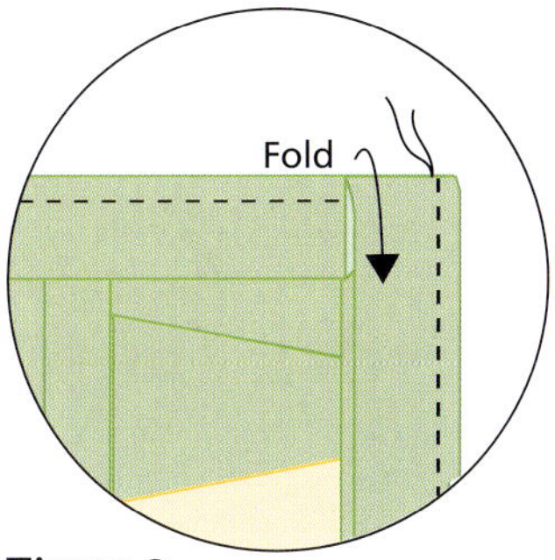

Figure 6

Figure 7

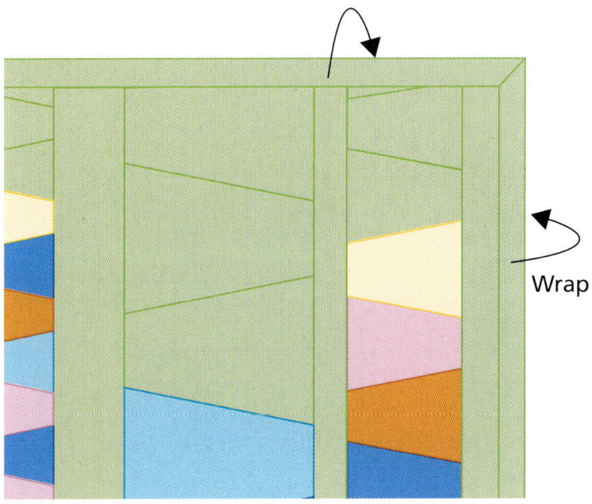

Figure 8

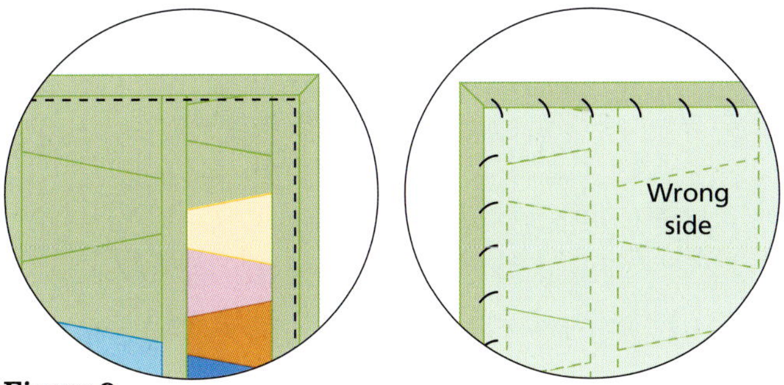

Figure 9

Patterns

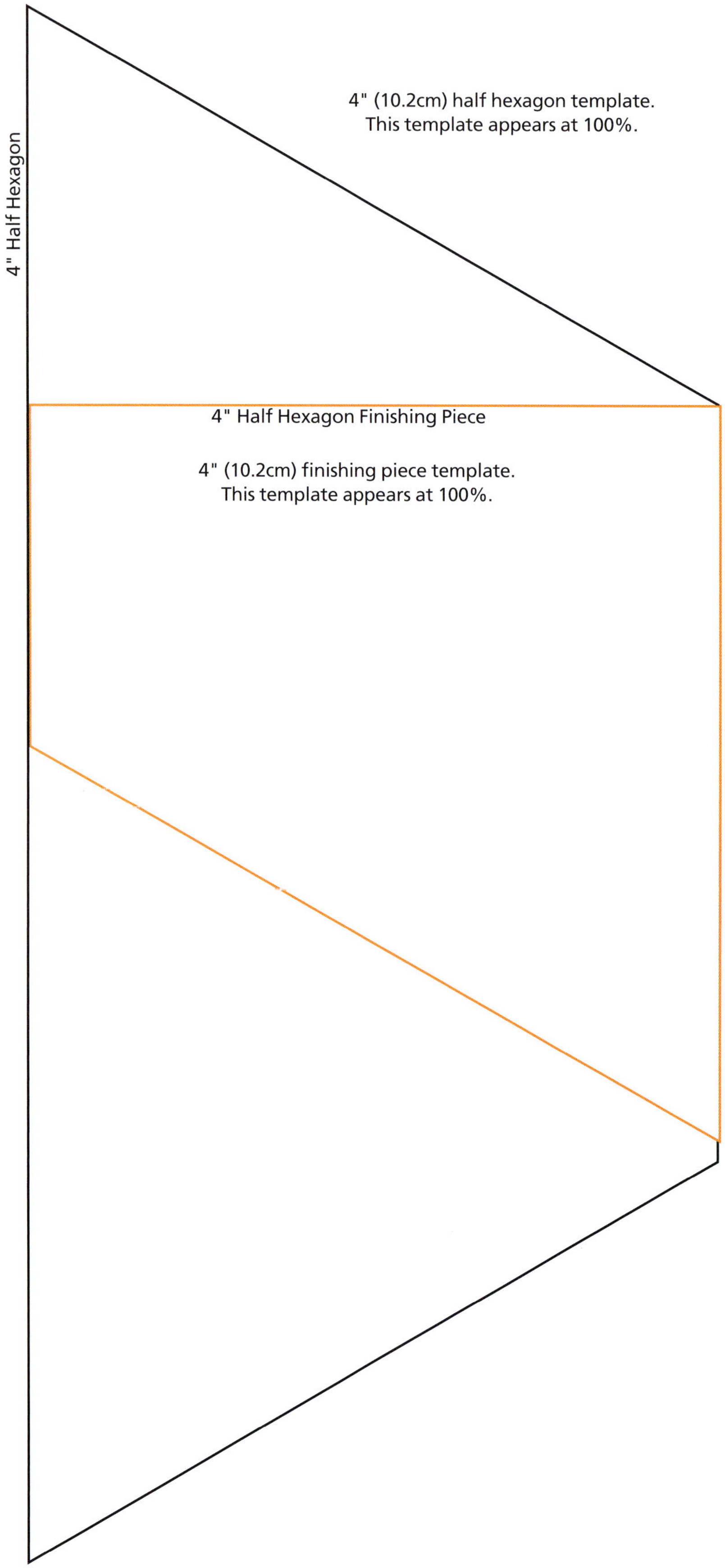

Templates for *Hit-and-Miss Table Runner*, page 64. The templates appear at full size.

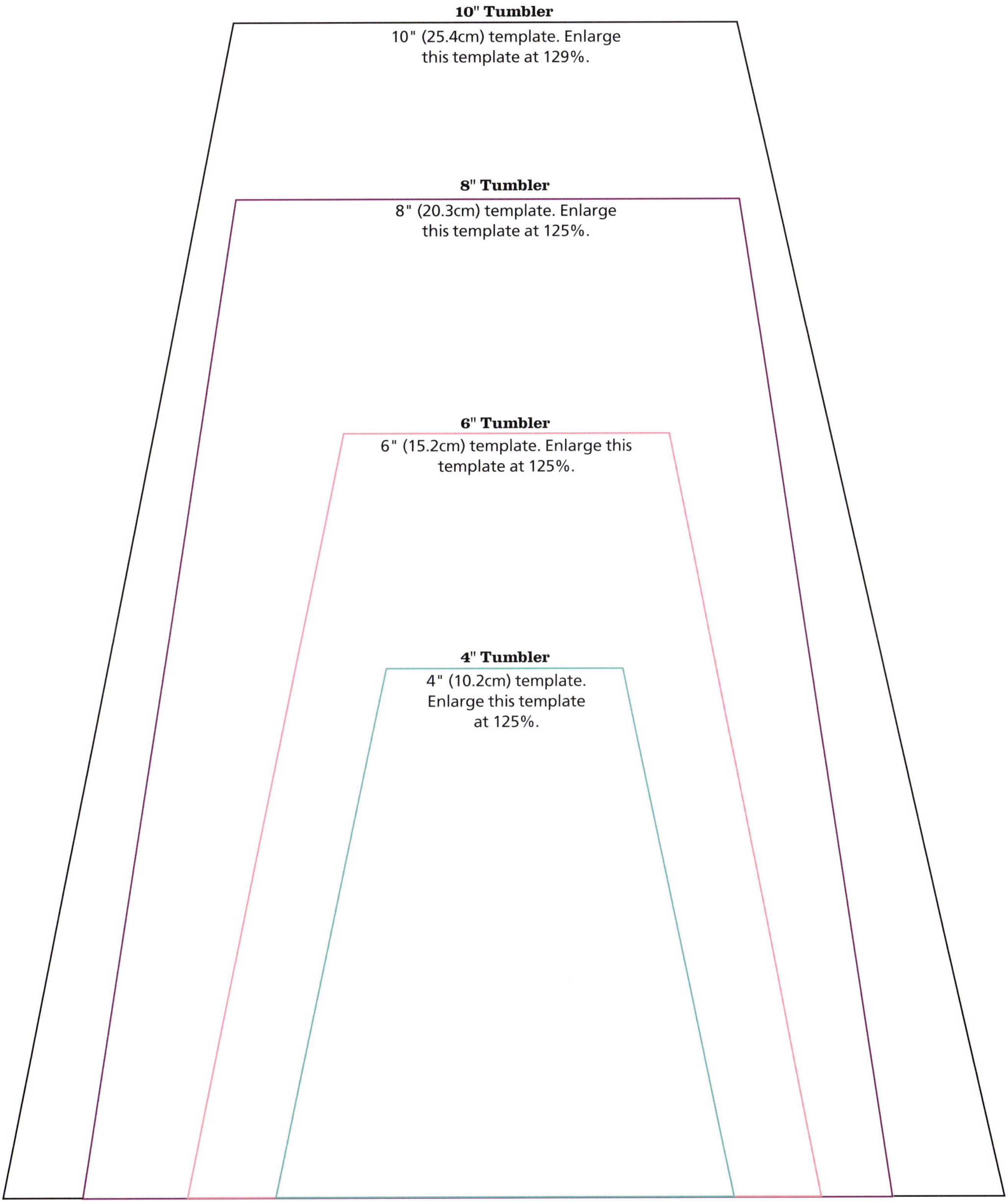

Templates for *Tumbling Tumblers Column Quilt*, page 70. Enlarge at percentages noted above to bring to full size.

Resources

The products used to create the projects in this book are available from your local quilt, fabric or craft store as well as from sewing catalogs and online retailers. If you are unable to find a product, contact the manufacturers below for more information.

Sewing Supplies and Notions

By Annie
www.byannie.com

Clover Needlecraft, Inc.
www.clover-usa-com

Coats & Clarks
www.makeitcoats.com/en-us

E-Z Quilting by Wrights
www.ezquilt.com

Gingher
www.gingher.com

Klassé Needles
www.klasse.com/en/

Mary Ellen Products
maryellenproducts.com

Little Foot Ltd.
littlefoot.net

OLFA
www.olfa.com

Oliso Irons
oliso.com

Omnigrid Rulers
dritz.com/brands/omnigrid/

Pellon Consumer Products
www.pellonideas.com

Prym Consumer USA, inc.
www.dritz.com

Rowenta Irons
www.rowenta.com

Schmetz Needles
www.schmetzneedles.com

Wrights
www.wrights.com

Fabric

Moda Fabrics
www.unitednotions.com/un_main.nsf/fabrics

Riley Blake Designs
www.rileyblakedesigns.com

Robert Kaufmann
www.robertkaufman.com

Michael Miller
www.unitednotions.com/un_main.nsf/fabrics

Thread

Madeira Thread
madeirausa.com

Superior Threads
www.superiorthreads.com

YLI Thread
www.ylicorp.com

Batting

Hobbs Quilt Batting
www.hobbsbatting.com

Mountain Mist
www.mountainmistlp.com

Quilter's Dream Batting
www.quiltersdreambatting.com

The Warm Company
www.warmcompany.com

Index

METRIC CONVERSION CHART

To convert	to	multiply by
Inches	Centimeters	2.54
Centimeters	Inches	0.4
Feet	Centimeters	30.5
Centimeters	Feet	0.03
Yards	Meters	0.9
Meters	Yards	1.1

Publisher: Amy Barrett-Daffin

Creative Director: Gailen Runge

Senior Editor: Roxane Cerda

Editors: Christine Doyle and Diane Dhein (Nancy's Notions editor)

Cover/Book Designer: Courtney Kyle

Production Coordinators: Greg Nock and Zinnia Heinzmann

Illustrator: Laure Noe

Photography by Nancy Armstrong, OMS Photography; Al Parrish

Published by C&T Publishing, Inc., P.O. Box 1456, Lafayette, CA 94549

Library of Congress Control Number: 2026933575

Printed in China

10 9 8 7 6 5 4 3 2 1

About the Author

Nancy Zieman—author, designer, businesswoman, producer, blogger and national sewing authority—is the host of the popular show *Sewing With Nancy*, which appears exclusively on public television stations across the United States and Canada. *Sewing With Nancy* is a co-production of Wisconsin Public Television and Nancy Zieman Productions. Broadcast since September 1982, the program is the longest-airing sewing series on television. Nancy organizes each show in a how-to format that concentrates on step-by-step instructions.

Nancy has written numerous books. She designs patterns for McCall Pattern Company, designs sewing and quilting products for Clover Needlecraft, Inc., and also writes an interactive blog found at nancyzieman.com/blog.

In addition, Nancy is founder of Nancy's Notions and the national spokesperson for Nancy's Notions and Baby Lock sewing machines.

Nancy lives in Beaver Dam, Wisconsin, with her husband, Richard. The couple has two children and two grandchildren.